FUNNY YOU SHOULD ASK

Weird But True Answers to 115$^{1/2}$ Wacky Questions

Marg Meikle

illustrated by **Tina Holdcroft**

Scholastic Canada Ltd.

D0206144

To Noel

Scholastic Canada Ltd.
175 Hillmount Road, Markham, Ontario, Canada L6C 1Z7

Scholastic Inc.
555 Broadway, New York, NY 10012, USA

Scholastic Australia Pty Limited
PO Box 579, Gosford, NSW 2250, Australia

Scholastic New Zealand Limited
Private Bag 94407, Greenmount, Auckland, New Zealand

Scholastic Ltd.
Villiers House, Clarendon Avenue, Leamington Spa,
Warwickshire CV32 5PR, UK

Cover and design by Andrea Casault

Canadian Cataloguing in Publication Data

Meikle, Margaret
Funny you should ask

ISBN 0-590-12489-7

1. Children's questions and answers. I. Title.
AG195.M454 1998   j031.02   C98-930685-2

Copyright © 1998 by Marg Meikle. All rights reserved.

No part of this publication may be reproduced or stored in a retrieval system, or
transmitted in any form or by any means, electronic, mechanical, recording, or
otherwise, without written permission of the publisher, Scholastic Canada Ltd.,
175 Hillmount Road, Markham, Ontario, Canada L6C 1Z7. In the case of
photocopying or other reprographic copying, a licence must be obtained from
CANCOPY (Canadian Copyright Licensing Agency),
1 Yonge Street, Suite 1900, Toronto, Ontario, Canada M5E 1E5.

8 7   Printed in Canada   3 4

Contents

How do flies land
on the ceiling?

and Other Amazing Answers About ANIMALS

How do flies land on the ceiling?

It helps to know that flies are a lot more like helicopters than planes. Flies can't fly parallel to the ceiling too well because their wings might touch it, but they can fly straight up or down as well as horizontally. Flies are very versatile aircraft.

A fly does something of a half loop to land on the ceiling. It is moving upward at a little over thirty centimetres per second. As it approaches the ceiling it puts all six of its legs out, with the front two sticking upward a bit. It extends those two legs above its head and they touch the ceiling first. When those legs make contact, the fly grabs on (insect legs are particularly good at this sort of thing on almost any surface). Then it rolls bellyward in a half-loop and the other four legs contact and adhere. The fly actually ends up facing the opposite direction from the way it was flying. To get off, it just drops down.

A fly is far more tolerant of gravity than humans. Humans can only withstand a gravitational (or G) force of 10; we would black out if we zipped up to the ceiling any quicker. A fly reaches a G force of about 200, and a jumping flea also reaches close to 200.

Flies are very light. It takes 10,000 of them to make 1 kilogram.

2.

If dogs are colour-blind, how do guide dogs know when to stop or go at a traffic light?

Guide dogs for the blind are working dogs. So are other assistance dogs, like hearing ear dogs, and those who assist people in wheelchairs. They are highly trained dogs, but just dogs nonetheless.

Working dogs like to play. Many of them are keen on romping in the snow or chasing a tennis ball, but for these dogs their job comes first. They guide their owners day in and day out, from landmark to landmark, stopping at stairs, curbs and intersections. This guiding is safe, much faster than walking with a cane, and inspires a lot more confidence.

Part of a guide dog's job is dealing with traffic. Traffic lights come in three colours, of course, but dogs can't tell green from red, or green and red from amber. So how do these colour-blind dogs deal with traffic lights? It turns out they don't watch traffic lights at all. Guide dogs are trained to stop at all intersections. They have to listen to the owners, who might want to turn right or left, so the dog waits for a command. If the person says Forward, the dog starts up, unless there is any traffic coming. If so, the dog won't move.

What if the light is red? If there is no traffic coming and the light is red the dog has no idea and just goes. When there is a traffic box that clicks, the dog can hear the clicking of the changing lights and know when to go. The new beeping crossings are great. There is one sound for north–south and a different sound for east–west, so the handler knows when it's safe to go.

Dogs aren't the only animals who are colour-blind. Most animals just see shades of grey. Birds and some fish see some colours, but the only animals that have the same range of colour vision as humans are apes and some of the higher monkeys.

3

Is it true that one "person year" is the same as seven "dog years"? How was this figured out, and does it work for other animals?

That 1:7 ratio of so-called human to dog years is an odd one, because how can we use "human years" on a dog? What we are doing is comparing the animal world to the human world, and it doesn't really work. (It doesn't stop us from trying though.)

Scientists originally came up with the 1:7 ratio by looking at the physical, sexual and social maturity of dogs, as well as information on their behaviour. What scientists figured out was that in the first year, a dog goes from birth to about the same stage as a fifteen-year-old person — physically, sexually and socially. Then in the second year it goes up to about twenty-four in human years. After that, the answer is: it depends. The ratio was averaged out to 1:7 because humans often live to around seventy and dogs to around ten.

So the 1:7 thing doesn't really work. It is more of a sliding scale. Most basic dog owner's manuals have a chart that averages the breeds and compares dog ages. Generally, dog people don't even like those ratios. Dogs are living much longer now than they used to because of excellent nutrition and better medical care. What works best is to just generalize about stages of life. By six months a dog is like a six-year-old child — ready to begin school. By one year a dog hits puberty and could reproduce, but isn't really ready. Two years is like young adulthood — dogs are physically mature but have lots of room for more mental maturity.

What about cats? Comparing with human ages

The ratio for the years also depends on the size of the dog. Big dogs like Great Danes and St. Bernards don't live as long, maybe eight to ten years. But smaller dogs, like all of the toy breeds, Miniature Poodles and Westies, have longer life expectancies of fourteen to sixteen years, so their age ratio would be different.

just isn't done. Mostly cat people just talk about life stages. An eight-year-old cat is in an early geriatric (old age) stage and a fourteen-year-old cat is definitely geriatric.

Zookeepers don't compare animal ages to human ages either. Part of the reason is that they look after animals with such different life spans. Elephants live to sixty years or so, and a lot of the small animals live only three or four years. If the animal came from the wild, the zoo doesn't know how old it was to begin with. Zookeepers look at the teeth for wear, but that comparison is only a guess because in the zoo the nutrition is often better and the animals lead an easier life than in the wild. So zoo staff mostly just figure out whether an animal is young, middle-aged or old.

How can chickens run around with their heads cut off?

Freshly decapitated chickens will flop around a lot. They will even run around with their heads cut off for a few seconds, flapping their wings wildly.

How does this happen? The adrenalin in the muscle tissue gives the bird convulsions, making it look like it is still alive. Chickens flap and flop around for about thirty seconds before they are totally dead. That flopping/flapping movement can carry the headless chicken along a few metres. The chicken isn't really running, but it looks like it is.

"Running around like a chicken with its head cut off" has become an expression we use about someone who is frenzied. We also call this going ape, having kittens, flipping your lid or blowing your stack. All of these expressions mean you are in a flap or in a dither, or excited, frantic and harried.

Do slugs have any purpose whatsoever, or do they just lie around looking slimy?

Slugs are one of a gardener's worst enemies. These pests chew up young plants and vegetables and eat holes in leaves. Controlling them is tedious and difficult. But these slimy creatures do have a greater purpose, and their own place in the food chain or ecosystem. Slugs are the original recyclers. They eat decaying vegetation, dead leaves, fungi, some animal feces, carrion and even other slugs. Slugs are then eaten by ground beetles or small mammals like voles and moles, or snakes, birds or beetles. So the circle of the natural world continues . . . in its own slimy way.

Why do dogs' and cats' eyes go a funny colour in photographs?

If you shoot all your pictures outside you won't have a problem. But use a flash and you've got the glowing-eye thing happening. If you don't have a pet, you probably thought that photography disasters were confined to the red eyes of humans. With humans this happens because you use a flash in a low-light setting, when the pupil of your eye is dilated (opened wider to let in more light so you can see even when it's dark). When the flash hits the eye, it bounces off the back of the retina and back out through the pupil of the eye. That red you notice is blood. You see a so-called "red reflex," which is really the red colour of the back of the eye, or the fundus, with all its blood vessels.

The new cameras have "red-eye reduction" which gives two flashes in a row. The first flash illuminates the fundus. By the time the second flash goes off, your pupil is still constricted from the first flash, so you don't get red in your photo.

This is similar to what happens with dogs and cats, but with dogs and cats you see a green glow. Their retinas are more complex. They have an area of reflective cells called *tapetum lucidum* on the topmost layer of the retina, which gives them the ability to see better in the dark than humans. So a flash photo or bright light reflects off the *tapetum*, which can be green or yellow or blue, producing that same greenish glow as when car headlights shine into an animal's eyes.

Huskies and collies with blue irises don't have this *tapetum*. You will notice that their photos turn out fine.

Tips to get good photos of your dog or cat
(without glowing eyes):

- Try to shoot outside. The grass also makes a nice backdrop.

- Use a flash bracket, or hold your flash off the camera. Direct on-camera flash gives the worst results.

- It helps if you can get the animal to look away. (Get a friend to redirect the animal's attention.)

- Turn up the room lights so the pupils will be smaller.

- Use your camera's red-eye reduction system, if you have one. Or use a grey-coloured dye pen which you touch to the photograph. The green eye tones down and looks natural. (There is a red-eye remover for humans too. Brilliant inventions.)

Why is a lion the "king of the jungle"? Lions don't even live in the jungle.

It's true, lions don't live in the jungle. Lions like grassy plains and open savannah. They live mostly in Africa, south of the Sahara Desert. There are also a few hundred lions living in the Gir Forest National Park in India.

Way back — from 1,500,000 years ago right up to 10,000 years ago — lions lived all over the world: in the Balkans, the Middle East and even all over North America. Some may even have lived in what is now your city! Slowly they disappeared from everywhere except Africa and India, and even there, lions are really surviving well only in the national parks.

The lion is probably regarded as the king of the animals because of its legendary ferocity, but why do people continue to think the lion is the king of the *jungle?*

It's a big mix-up from history. Jungle means overgrown land. And back before TV and air travel, when people learned about the world from a few travel writings, the word got out that all of Africa was a savage and wild jungle. Certainly parts of Africa are a jungle, but the English figured it all was.

Tarzan was a big part of the problem (or Edgar Rice Burroughs, who wrote the Tarzan books). Tarzan, or King of the Apes and Lord of the Jungle, lived in Africa — at least, that's where the books are set. In the very first book, Tarzan kills a tiger. OOPS! Tigers live in India. The Tarzan books also show the lion as a jungle beast who lives alone. They ought to show the lion as an animal in charge of a pride (a group of female lions and their cubs) that lives on the grassy plains. However, the fact that this information was wrong didn't seem to hurt book and movie sales.

There are no lions in *The Jungle Book* by Rudyard Kipling, or in the movie by Disney. Good thing, since the story takes place in a tropical jungle in India. The Disney movie *The Lion King* got it right too. The movie begins with the lions roaming the savannah, but the action shifts to the jungle when Simba runs away from the evil Uncle Scar. Simba is amazed with the jungle and feels very out of place there. He knows, as you do now, that lions belong on the plains.

Do chickens have lips?

Not really. Chickens have nothing soft like our lips, just a hard beak. Since there is no such thing as chicken lips, it's simply a weird expression that means "something imaginary." It's kind of like saying "horsefeathers" to mean nonsense. If somebody serves you a dish called chicken lips, they're just having fun.

Why do zebras have black and white stripes?

Camouflage is the obvious answer, but where is there a black and white forest or jungle? Tigers blend in with their stripes in tall grasses, but zebras really stand out. What was the point of Mother Nature painting these elegant creatures in black and white?

The animals that prey on zebras are busiest during the cool hours of sunrise and sunset. It turns out that the black and white stripes show up as grey from a distance, which helps the zebras blend in with the low light.

And the other reason, which is very cool, is that if a zebra herd gets attacked, the wildly moving jagged stripes of the whole herd of zebras confuse the predator.

So there you go. Colour isn't everything when it comes to camouflage.

Seagulls' colouring works so they *can* be seen. Seagulls are white so that other seagulls can see when one gull is eating . . . and realize that there's good fishing. That's why gulls usually attract other gulls.

Why do we forget?

and Other Fascinating Bits About Your BODY

Why do you close your eyes when you sneeze?

It's a reflex. Your eyes snap shut when you sneeze, and it's pretty much impossible to keep them open. The nerves serving the eyes and the nose are very closely connected. If you stimulate one nerve, like in your nose when you sneeze, often it will trigger some response in the other. It's like having your eyes water when you yawn.

There's a kids' rumour or an old wives' tale that if you keep your eyes open when you sneeze, your eyes will pop out. But it's just a tale. Even if you could keep your eyes open, they wouldn't pop out.

Sneezing is just an extreme form of breathing. When you sneeze, air is exhaled violently through your nasal passages. So why do we sneeze? To keep foreign material out of the body. If you inhale particles like dust, the tiny particles will excite your nose and trigger a sneeze. You'll sneeze if you have a cold too, or if you have allergies.

Some people sneeze when they go out into the bright sunlight. That's called the photic sneeze reflex. It happens to sixteen to twenty-five per cent of the population. It is also genetic — you have a sixty-four per cent chance of inheriting it if one of your parents is a photic sneezer.

We sneeze for other reasons too. Pepper and strong-smelling things like ammonia, or strong-tasting things like hot chilies, don't trigger our smell or taste senses. The receptors that respond are pain receptors, and the response is a reflex to protect us from inhaling something dangerous.

The particles ejected in a forceful sneeze have been clocked at 166 kilometres per hour.

The most chronic fit of sneezing was by Donna Griffiths of Pershore, England. She caught a cold and started sneezing on January 13, 1981 . . . and stopped 978 days later. She likely sneezed about a million times in the first year alone, and made it into the *Guinness Book of Records*.

Do you really get only one set of eyelashes? And why do lashes stay one length when other hair keeps growing?

No, eyelashes keep getting replaced. They grow as long as they need to be to do their job. What's their job? Eyelashes are a bit like nose hair. Eyelashes are there to keep dust and sweat and dirt and bugs and airborne particles out of your eyes. They are also designed to protect your eyes from the glare of the sun.

The eyelid protects the eyeball, and the eyelashes are responsible for screening matter out of the eye. If anything comes toward the eye and the very sensitive eyelashes, or if anything moves suddenly, the lids blink hard by reflex, to protect the eyeball. When you blink by reflex, the eyeball is quickly washed with a coat of tears and mucus to clean it off. That keeps it healthy and moving properly. We blink every two to ten seconds, and all of this happens without us even noticing.

Where do you go to the bathroom in an igloo?

First of all, you have to let go of the idea that you need a flush toilet to be able to go to the bathroom. It takes running water to make a toilet flush, but in the far North when igloos were used as homes, there was no running water. The people who used igloos had a different idea that worked just as well.

Igloos or dome-shaped snow houses come in two styles: large winter residential dwellings and small, hastily constructed hunters' huts for single-night stays. The big winter house was actually a series of snowdomes connected by passageways. Fifteen to twenty people lived inside, reclining on skins spread on the floor, and on low platforms. The temperature was always around freezing.

No one has really lived in these winter homes since the 1950s, although hunting huts are still used. Both structures are built in spirals from within, using blocks of snow, which makes great insulation.

We know about bathrooms in igloos because of a Danish explorer, Therkel Mathiassen. He was a member of the Fifth Thule Expedition (1921– 1924) and wrote about igloos in *Material Culture of the Iglulik Eskimos*. "The largest single snow house I have seen was lined with skin and measured 18 feet [5.5 m] in diameter, and 8 feet [2.5 m] high. There was a central store room, from which were doors to the house, to two smaller side rooms for clothing and meat, and a wooden door to the dogs' room, in one side of which was a small opening into a separate little snow house which acted as a latrine."

At the time, urine was collected in large urine tubs for use in preparing animal skins. The ammonia in urine cuts grease, so the Inuit also used it to wash hair and clothes.

The single-night hunting igloos are another story. Usually about four hunters travel together and make an igloo two metres in diameter. That's close quarters. The floors are covered with caribou skins. Men can pull back the caribou skin and urinate onto the floor of snow. The warm urine burns a hole into the snow and freezes. It's a little trickier for women, who lean against the wall, peel back the skins from the floor and urinate. It's all very clean.

How do you go to the bathroom in space?

This is the question most often asked of NASA. That's no surprise. There is no gravity at all up there, but people still have a biological need to expel fluid. The possibilities for disaster are endless. Astronauts go to the bathroom like we do, because every Space Shuttle has one toilet for both men and women. It is sort of like ours. But in outer space, air is used instead of flowing water to remove waste. And you have to sit really firmly on the seat to make sure that nothing floats up.

Then the astronauts compress the solid wastes and store them onboard until they can be removed after landing. Because of how liquids react in zero gravity, the moisture in the solids sort of boils away quickly. The air is filtered to get rid of the odour and bacteria, and then returned to the cabin.

A space toilet is not simple, and it's not cheap. Just one costs around $24 million dollars (U.S.) By the way, astronauts brush their teeth just like we do on earth. And there is no shower on the Shuttle, so astronauts must make do with sponge baths until they return home.

What makes someone an albino?

People and animals born with no colouring at all in their hair, eyes or skin are albinos. Animals, plants, and people from any racial group can be albino — they lack the pigment or colouring matter that most of us have. Pigments come in lots of shades: for example blue, brown, or green eyes; the wild feathers of a parrot or the stripes of a zebra or a tabby cat. Skin gets colour from a dark pigment called melanin. Caucasians, or white people, have less melanin than black people do. Albinos have no melanin at all. Their skin tends to look quite pink, because their blood vessels are showing through. Their hair is snow white. Albino people need to wear sunglasses in the sun because their eyes have no pigment for protection from very strong light. (For this same reason you will find that people with blue eyes want to put on sunglasses sooner than people with brown eyes, because they have less pigment in their eyes.)

Colouring is passed on from your parents through your genes. Albinos also inherit their lack of colour. Some albino parents might have children who are not albinos, but those same children might later go on to produce albinos. Or it might not happen again for many generations.

There are also albino plants. They lack chlorophyll, the green food material. With no food, albino plants quickly die.

Freckles are just little round spots — concentrations of the skin pigment called melanin. Some people get them when they go out in the sun, others live freckle-free. And kids get freckles far more than adults.

16

Why do old people shrink?

Shrink sounds like a strong term, but it is true. Old people lose height and muscle and fat, so they get smaller. Their spines begin to degenerate and compress, making them shorter. That's partially gravity taking hold. We all get shorter in the course of a day because water gets squeezed out of the discs of the spine. However, it is permanent in older people because there is less water in the discs to start with. Younger people have more water to begin with, and spring back to height at night.

Add to this the fact that the vertebrae can crush as you get older because of a condition called osteoporosis. People with osteoporosis have bones that aren't dense enough to hold their weight. Some older people also can't stand up straight — they stoop because of the crushed vertebrae.

Almost everything to do with shrinkage relates to diet and exercise. So get lots of exercise, fresh air and good food with plenty of calcium. That way you will have done your part to stay as big and strong as possible. The total amount you will shrink depends on how much you stay in shape. Generally, a man might lose three centimetres, and a woman five centimetres, between ages thirty to seventy.

Why do we have nose hair?

Your nose hair is simply a filter to clean up the air you breathe. It is there so that any small bits of dirt and dust trapped in the mucus coating the nose hair won't make it into your lungs. Nose hairs are called *vibrissae*. If you ever go to a very polluted city, you will find that when you blow your nose the tissue looks like a filter from a dryer or pool — full of dirt! The nose hair has to work extra hard to keep you healthy.

The scary part is how older men sometimes have extra-long nose hair sticking out from their noses. This has spawned an industry of some pretty weird appliances, like electric nose-hair clippers.

Why do we forget?

Actually, there is no evidence that we ever forget anything. It is all in your brain somewhere. But remembering is like trying to find something in your room when it is a big mess. The key to retrieving information from your brain, just like finding your shoes in your messy room, is in how we organize our thoughts (or our stuff!). And with memory, the trick is to teach ourselves how to remember things. So when people say their memory is going, what is really happening is that their retrieval system isn't working well.

Everyone has different methods of learning. Some people need to hear someone explain something, others need to draw themselves a diagram or read it for themselves.

If you want to remember something, you first have to learn and understand it, and consciously think of a cue for when you will want to remember it. How you do this depends on your learning style and the method of retrieval that works best for you.

There are loads of books and courses on improving your memory. Some of the basic ideas include coming up with a trick or a mnemonic to help you remember something. You have to tell yourself how to remember this person or this thing. Maybe you will connect a name to a physical feature, like deciding that the man you met called Chuck Brown has a round head like Charlie Brown, and Chuck is a short form for Charlie.

Maybe a corny verse would help:

I before E
Except after C,
Or in rhyming with A,
As in neighbour and weigh.

You might need to say something out loud twice, or write it down so you can see the word. Or maybe you have to sing it to yourself. These are all cues you are setting up. Everything is in your brain somewhere, it just takes the right cue to get it out. So if you really want to remember something, figure out what will work for you when you store it.

To remember the notes of the treble-clef lines of music:

Every Good Boy Deserves Fudge (E, G, B, D, F)

The notes of the bass-clef lines are:
Girls Buy Dolls For Amusement (G, B, D, F, A)

To remember the Great Lakes, say HOMES:

Huron, Ontario, Michigan, Erie and Superior

To remember how to set clocks when daylight-saving time starts and finishes:

Spring forward, fall back.

What happens to all the chewing gum we swallow? Does it stick up our insides?

Although it's not exactly digestible, gum doesn't usually stay in your stomach for seven years, as the old saying goes. It makes its way out, just like everything else you put in your mouth and swallow. But several cases where small children have clogged their digestive tracts by swallowing a lot of gum have been reported, so you're better just to chew, not swallow.

Why were people smaller in the old days?

Why? Nutrition. In the old days (not even 100 years ago for many places) people ate mostly what they could grow and put away, so their nutrition would depend on where they were farming or what they could buy or barter. We've got better food now, but more than that, we have methods of preserving our foods by refrigeration and other techniques. We can eat anything all year long, because we can now transport food around the world. This improved nutrition, including more protein, often makes for bigger babies and children.

Here's something else to think about. Folks "back then" were considered normal sized for their time. It is just that the next generations have gotten bigger and bigger!

Why do men have Adam's apples?

That lump on men's necks, the outer part of the voice box or larynx, is called an Adam's apple. Women have one too, but a man's Adam's apple is at a sharper angle and seen more easily.

The Adam's apple is named after Adam, who the Bible says was one of the first two people on the earth (along with Eve, his mate). The legend is that Adam ate some forbidden fruit from the Garden of Eden and a piece of it got stuck in his throat. That throat bulge has been with men forever, supposedly to show that men can be weak and give in to temptation.

The medical explanation is that men have stronger larynx muscles, hence deeper voices, and the Adam's apple is where those muscles are stored.

Vegetarians tend to be smaller than people who eat a lot of meat. But bigger isn't always better, since smaller creatures may live longer — but right now the only evidence of this comes from animal research.

Can you really drink your urine?

The answer is yes, you can, and some people do. But the question is, would you really want to?

People drink their urine for a variety of reasons. It is an ancient practice, and the people who do it claim that it helps their health by boosting their immune system. There are many stories about drinking one's own urine bringing miraculous cures from awful diseases. Urine therapy is particularly popular in India and in Germany. It is called the Water of Life or Life Elixir.

This is why people drink urine: They think that when the kidney makes urine it takes excess vital parts out of your blood along with the water that needs to pass through. They think that urine is not simply waste, but is full of nutrients, hormones, enzymes and antibodies that are filtered out of the blood. It is also believed that morning urine is the richest and the best for you.

If this really grosses you out, there is one time when you had better get over it. Say you are stranded in the middle of the ocean on a life raft, or in the middle of the desert in extreme heat. No water means dehydration, even death. So go for it. This is survival, and drinking your urine can save your life.

Did men really wear high heels?

and Other Strange Facts About CLOTHES

Why is it impolite for boys and men to wear a hat indoors, but not for a woman?

It's all about history. These days, some students may wear hats to school — it is up to the individual school district. But wearing hats indoors has been mostly limited to women.

A lot of the hats we wear are functional — to keep our ears warm, or to keep the sun off. Sometimes hats are simply a fashion statement: "I am conventional," or "I am flamboyant." Then there are the hats that are symbols of something else. Think about it — anyone with power tends to wear a head covering, and any ceremony usually involves hats. Queens and kings wear hats. The military, ministers and rabbis, brides and graduates wear symbolic head coverings (although throughout history it was more common than now). Hats were also symbols of class and status. Up until the eighteenth century most of the posing to do with hats was a male game. Think of Napoleon Bonaparte. He had a hat that said, "Look at me, I have an important position!"

Since men wore hats for symbolic reasons, they have also had most of the rules about manners pointed at them. The rules have traditionally said that men must always take off their hats when they come indoors unless it is a place of worship where you must have your head covered.

Why? Part of this is also about men and their tendency, historically, to fight. If you uncovered your head, it showed respect. A knight would doff his helmet to show he relied on the protection of his host as long as he remained under his host's roof. A king expected knights to show respect for the throne by uncovering their heads when he arrived. It showed the chain of power — only the king didn't doff. Women have always had more leeway because women have been more peaceable.

The biggest rule for either male or female: Don't wear your hat in a theatre and block the view of others!

23.

How did it come about that men wore pants and women wore skirts? Didn't "cave people" all dress alike?

It's about function, purely and simply. Long past the cave men's times, men and women both wore a form of skirt. Egyptian men wore a form of loin skirt. Romans wore tunics and togas. These are all variations on a basic wrapped cloth. Men continued wearing various forms of "skirts" or robes, short or long, well into the fifteenth century.

Of course there are exceptions, which are mostly about work and labour divisions. Since Roman times, men figured out that although robes and skirts were comfortable and simple, they weren't very practical. The custom of men wearing pants had to do with their work roles as soldiers, nomads, farmers, riders and hunters. (An exception to this involves Scottish men wearing kilts — heavy wool skirts — for everything.)

In some societies there was also a keen interest in keeping women unable to work or fight. Women's wearing of trousers is a very recent innovation in most cultures — less than fifty years in most places.

Why didn't women get trousers? There is a practical answer to this question. A skirt or "dress" is easy to make — two flat pieces of fabric with two simple seams. Even easier, a sarong or toga is just a woven piece of fabric that's then wrapped around the body. Trousers are much more difficult to sew than dresses, so they were only made when needed for men's work. In fact, a lot of men today who sit at desks or who do jobs that aren't physically strenuous might be quite happy to wear a robe or skirt if that fashion ever came back!

Is it true that men were the first to wear high heels?

Yes, it is true. You wouldn't believe what men used to wear on their feet. Men's shoes today are truly boring. Back in the twelfth century, in Europe, men wore shoes called *crackows* or *poulaines*, with long pointed toes. Sometimes the wealthy wore these shoes up to sixty centimetres long, although the average citizen only wore fifteen-centimetre points. These shoes were made of soft leather, so wooden clogs called pattens were worn below the shoes to protect them.

Then about 400 years later shoe styles for both men and women went to low-cut, square-toed slippers. People got crazy with the toes, rolling them back and even slashing the leather to show the coloured lining. The toes got so wide that a law came out to limit the size.

High heels came in during the late sixteenth century. It was Louis XIV of France who really popularized them. He was a short monarch who wanted to be taller. (Even today a curved heel is called a French, or Louis, heel.) These were floppy shoes with square toes and long tongues, fastened with buckles or big bows. Men also wore wide-topped boots that were soft leather, and often shoes with really loose lacy hose. If you can picture the cat in *Puss in Boots*, that's the kind of boots we're talking about.

Shoemakers moved on to using stiffer leather in the eighteenth century so they could make higher boots, and high-heeled buckled shoes with pointed toes. The middle of the nineteenth century saw shoes beginning to be mass-manufactured, making them affordable to the general public. Mass manufacturing also meant shoes weren't as specialized anymore, and men's shoes today are certainly not as fancy as they once were.

Why are my jeans more comfortable than anything else I wear?

Blue jeans started out back in the 1870s as clothing for miners and cowboys in the United States. Here's how it happened. Levi Strauss followed the miners to California during the big gold rush, thinking he would sell them tent canvas. He quickly found out there was a much greater need for sturdy work pants, so he used the heavy fabric for what he called "waist overalls" or "great pants." These pants were good for work wear because they were strong and long lasting. Levi Strauss also figured out how to rivet the corners of pockets so that they couldn't rip.

Eventually the fabric for the pants changed to blue denim. Some say it's called denim because it is the serge or strong twill fabric from Nîmes, France, or in French: *de Nîmes. De Nîmes* became denim. Eventually Strauss dyed the denim blue, and the name "great pants" or *genes* became jeans. But jeans were still practical, not cool. Cool came along in the 1950s as movie actors James Dean, Marlon Brando and others wore blue jeans.

So the cool, the young and the rebels began to wear jeans, and now everyone does. Why? The sturdiness means that once you have a pair broken in, you know that these pants aren't going to wear out right away. Unlike other clothes that get washed out and limp as they get older, denim gets softer and more comfortable the more you wash and wear it, because of the flexible properties of the twill weave. The colour gets nicer as it fades, too. No wonder jeans are everyone's favourite clothes.

26. Why did women wear white gloves for formal occasions?

Gloves have been around for a long time. It makes sense. Your hands get cold, or need protection from heavy work, so you cover them. Gloves have been found in an Egyptian tomb from around 1350 B.C.

By the Middle Ages (the fifth to fifteenth centuries) gloves went from purely functional to highly decorative, and were worn by royalty, the rich, the powerful and church officials. More functional armoured gloves were worn for hunting or fighting. In the thirteenth century women began wearing ornamental elbow-length gloves.

A whole language of symbolism started to develop around gloves. If you threw down a glove it challenged someone to battle. If a knight or soldier picked it up the challenge was accepted. If you gave someone a folded glove it meant you would carry out a contract in good faith. A lady often gave a glove as a love token. Since gloves were most often given as gifts, they were high-status objects and often, in the Elizabethan era, they were held, not worn.

Then the white glove thing got started. By the nineteenth century wearing white gloves was considered proper for ladies, in order that their hands would not touch others', particularly those of men when shaking hands, dancing and so on. White gloves were part of formal wear. Because white gloves are hard to keep clean, they indicated a woman of superior social class, a woman who probably didn't do her own cleaning — she was above that, and could go around wearing white gloves. Although gloves used to be worn for all formal occasions, you rarely see them anymore as part of a dressed-up outfit.

Why do women's blouses open on the opposite side from men's shirts?

Women's button right over left, men's left over right. But why? There are loads of theories, but no absolute answer. Of course these theories all favour right-handed people or at least acknowledge that more people are right- than left-handed.

Originally all clothes hooked or clasped or buttoned right over left (the women's way). Then something happened to make men's closures go the other way. Buttoning left over right is supposed to be easier for right-handed people. History says that a man could adjust his shirt (or pants) with the left hand while keeping the right hand warm in his pocket. That left his right hand free to grab the sword that he wore on his left side. It's all about self-defence — and it has carried on. Women's clothing stayed with the original right-over-left method.

There is also a theory that had something to do with women and their dressers. No, not the dressers that you put clothes in, but the personal maid who would help you dress. If you are standing in front of someone and buttoning them up, it is easier to button from right to left, so according to this theory, that is why women's clothes button the way they do.

Another theory is that women would carry children in their left arm and use their right hand to unbutton their blouses for breast-feeding. But since women nurse their babies from both breasts, this theory is pretty lame.

28. Why are wedding rings worn on the third finger of the left hand?

Marriage is a downright prehistoric tradition. Wedding rings date from ancient Egypt. It was thought that there was a vein of blood running from the third finger of the left hand directly to the heart, called *vena amoris* or the vein of love. So the wedding ring should be worn on that love finger.

Why wear rings at all? The ring is a never-ending circle, a simple, unbroken band that is meant to signify the continuity of your love, even after death. The Egyptians wore rings made of bone, ivory, reeds or leather. Nowadays most of us wear rings of gold or silver, and diamonds or other gems are often inset into women's engagement or wedding bands.

Can humans spontaneously combust?

and Other Weird But COOL STUFF

29.

Can humans really spontaneously combust?

First things first. What exactly is spontaneous human combustion? It's when someone literally burns up for no obvious reason. You've probably seen something like it on shows like *The X-Files*.

But does it really happen? Over the last 400 years, there have been more than 200 cases reported. Charles Dickens even wrote about spontaneous human combustion in 1853 in his book, *Bleak House*.

Most of the reported cases seem to involve old people living in England — the sort who sit around in armchairs a lot. Reports usually describe the bodies as being very badly destroyed. In some cases there may be a limb or two left intact — a hand or maybe a foot. Sometimes there might even be a slipper still on the foot. Apparently, spontaneous combustion leaves behind a greasy-smelling sooty mess, but causes no damage to items right near the body. If someone were sitting in a chair in front of the television, the person would be a pile of soot. However, the television and the chair would be fine except for the burn mark on the seat of the chair. Go figure.

It's pretty gross and pretty unbelievable, but reports keep coming in. What people can't figure out is whether a fire has somehow been set outside the body. Scientists figure that there must be a cigarette or a fireplace accident that sets people on fire. True believers say otherwise. However, you should know that people rarely actually see spontaneous human combustion happen — just what's left behind.

Do eelskin wallets really demagnetize credit cards?

I hate to be the bearer of bad news, but this is an urban myth (something everyone regards as true, but really isn't). It is widespread, but a myth nonetheless. Eelskin does come from eels, but the skin doesn't have anything to do with electricity. Muscles make eels "electric," and when the eel dies, the electricity dies too.

There are two magnetic forces present in many wallets. A bank or credit card has a magnetic strip, a fine layer of oxide with tiny tracks on it like a computer disc. Information such as a person's name and account number is digitally encoded in that strip. The other magnet is on the magnetic clasp on the wallet. Eelskin leather is so delicate that manufacturers almost always use magnets rather than snaps for the wallet clasps. When a credit card magnet runs across the strong magnet in the clasp, that reaction wipes out the information on it. Banks hear about this a lot. The bank will tell you to get a plastic sleeve to store your cards in so that the magnetic areas don't touch, or to get a new wallet.

Sometimes though, you will hear about cards being demagnetized in wallets with no magnetic clasp. It could be just wear and tear on the cards, but there is a new theory. Korea has over-fished the eels whose skins are used for wallets. The eels used to be ten by sixty centimetres, but now they are pencil-sized. It costs the same to tan the small skins as the large ones, so now tanners also use the huge hagfish, or slime eel. (It is called that because it has big pores that ooze slime and oil.) The theory is that hagfish, even after tanning, secrete slime. Maybe that slime demagnetizes cards. This is one theory. Another is that metallic residue left over from the tanning process could be causing the reaction.

What's the story on the yo-yo?

31.

Yo-yos were invented in China around 1000 B.C. A yo-yo was a simple spinning toy made of two ivory disks and a silk cord. Yo-yos were also around in ancient Greece. A Greek vase that dates to 500 B.C., in the Berlin Museum, shows a painting of a boy playing with a yo-yo. There are workable yo-yos in the National Museum in Athens that are made from joined ceramic discs.

That's not all. In the Philippines yo-yos were used as weapons as far back as prehistoric days. The "yo-yo" was made of heavy hunks of flint attached to long leather thongs. The hunter would wait in a tree for his prey to pass by. He either knocked it out with the yo-yo, or tangled the thong around the animal's neck like a bola. If he missed he could try again because the yo-yo came back.

Yo-yos were also popular in the 1790s in Europe. There are paintings of monarchs like England's young King George yo-yoing, for example.

Adults loved yo-yos, and there were clubs that staged contests. Back then yo-yos were called *emigrette* or *joujou*. The English called them *incroyable, bandolore*, quiz or Prince of Wales's toy. *Joujou* might be where yo-yo comes from, although it is also the word for "come back" in Tagalog, the language of the Philippines.

Yo-yos came to North America in 1866, but it wasn't until Donald F. Duncan saw them in 1928 that the yo-yo craze took off. Duncan hired incredible champions who went to schoolyards and neighbourhoods to demonstrate the yo-yo and its charms. There were competitions and prizes, championship arm patches and tin pins. The heyday of yo-yoing was the Depression. Because the toys were inexpensive it was the perfect pastime. Even today there are a dozen or so freelance yo-yo pros in the U.S. One is a grandmother and another is a teenage girl. Get practising!

How does a lava lamp work?

You mean how do you get those big globs of goo slowly moving around inside glass globes filled with coloured liquid? A lava lamp works in mysterious ways.

Craven Walker invented lava lamps or lights in England in 1963. First he called it an animated motion mood lamp. Then he showed it at a trade fair in 1965 as the Astrolight. Adolph Wertheimer, a clever entrepreneur, bought the American manufacturing rights and started to manufacture them as TV lights — sort of an adult night light. The ads said: "A motion for every emotion." It sounds corny now, but in 1965 the Age of Aquarius folks were very keen for things psychedelic.

So what is that floating goop? It's a wax mixture. The lamp works like this: A forty-watt bulb heats the liquid and the waxy glob expands until it becomes less dense than the liquid surrounding it. (Less dense means the wax will float and rise.) When the globs get to the top of the globe, farther from the heat source, the wax cools again, contracts, gets heavy and starts to sink. The cycle repeats as the wax gets light and rises, gets heavy and sinks. Because of the nature of the waxy substance, as well as floating and sinking it also changes shape at the same time.

Of course it isn't as simple as just wax and water. There are apparently eleven secret ingredients mixed in vats in the Chicago manufacturing plant. They are carefully matched so that the wax doesn't break up into tiny bits and stay that way. You could say that the "glob factor" is the key to a great lava lamp.

Why were left-handed people considered evil?

and Other Crazy Answers About CUSTOMS

Why were left-handed people considered "evil" and forced to become right-handed?

Weird, huh? Even the Latin word for left, *sinister*, now has an association with the words bad or evil. At one time everything left was considered bad. That is because it wasn't "right" — people thought it just wasn't natural. So it is very important to put your right foot forward when entering a house, going on stage, or starting to walk. Considering anything to do with the left hand as both unlucky and evil is one of those nasty blanket superstitions that's especially hard on the ten per cent of men and eight per cent of women who are left-handed.

Left-handers have an advantage when fighting, which might be why right-handers have been so suspicious of them. This goes way back to medieval times. The spiral staircases in castles back then would coil clockwise (going downstairs). The story goes that the direction was set so the knights defending the castle could easily swing their swords about when coming *down* the stairs, while the attackers would have a problem swinging their swords coming *up* the stairs. But wait . . . this works only if both the attacker and the defender were right-handed. So if a lefty was attacking, he might win over a righty defending.

This lefty advantage carries on in sports today. Lefties do very well in sports where you confront your opponent face to face, as in fencing, tennis, boxing, cricket, ping-pong or baseball. Since so many people are right-handed, facing a lefty can throw them off their game.

How come people who are in love always give chocolates, and why is chocolate associated with Valentine's Day?

Nobody ate chocolates until the nineteenth century, when a British chocolate maker figured out how to make chocolate smooth and velvety. As a drink though, it was hot stuff in Mexico and Spain. In 1519 when Cortés showed up in Mexico, he found the Aztec Empire run by Emperor Montezuma, who was probably the original chocoholic. Montezuma drank litres of it every day out of golden goblets. It was thicker than our hot chocolate, dyed red, and had a chili-pepper flavour.

Cortés conquered the Aztecs, but hated the chocolate drink until he took cacao beans back to Spain and figured out how to add sugar and spices instead of chili peppers.

So what's the connection with love? Montezuma believed that chocolate made him very appealing to his harem of wives, which likely started the rumour of chocolate's connection with love . . . and eventually associated it with the day that celebrates lovers, Valentine's Day.

It's actually a chemistry thing. Just like coffee and tea, chocolate can fool with your brain. The theobromine (giving a mild caffeine-like buzz) and the magnesium (which comes in some tranquilizers and calms you down) give the chocolate eater a pleasant sensation. Chocolate isn't proven to make you more ready for love, but it tastes great and makes you feel good. What more could anyone ask for?

Why do people salute by putting their hands to their foreheads?

It is not entirely clear why, but there are some good theories. Back in ancient Europe it was common for people to carry arms or weapons. The custom was that men coming toward each other must lift their right hand to show that they had no intention of using their sword. That is likely how a number of friendly gestures got started, like tipping a hat, saluting, waving, or shaking the right hands. All of these gestures say: "This is peace, we're not going to fight you."

By the time of the Roman Empire salutes were part of the whole formality of the military. The salute at that time involved putting your right hand up to shoulder height with the palm out. The head wasn't touched yet — it was just a sort of tight-elbowed wave.

When knights who were wearing steel armour would ride up to each other, if they recognized the other knight or just wanted to display friendship, they would raise their visors to expose their faces. The knights held the reins in their left hand and did the visor lift with their right hand.

One form of salute we still use is doffing your hat to a superior. The hand moves up to the vicinity of the hat, but the hat isn't actually removed.

In the military, a subordinate salutes an officer and the officer must then return the salute. It is all about respect and discipline. In the military, a salute is absolutely compulsory, unlike the common but non-compulsory custom of shaking hands among the general public.

A wave is a kind of salute, as is the thumbs-up gesture ("All is well" or "It's okay"). Doffing your hat, kissing a person's hand, kissing both cheeks, shaking a hand or curtsying are all forms of greetings or salutes. None of these have the stand-up-straight quality of the military salute though, which is most impressive to watch.

The military and scouts aren't the only ones who salute or make a salute-like greeting as a sign of respect. Martial artists commonly salute with a bow when greeting each other, as a mutual show of respect for each other's skills and abilities. That salute had a practical application too. Martial artists were very cautious in the old days, and a handshake or a raising of the hand was considered either too threatening or an invitation for attack. So the bow works.

Why are there crescent moons on outhouse doors?

That's a good question. Why not full moons or stars or even square windows? The window is to let air and light in, obviously, and also for decoration. But why a crescent moon?

At one time the doors to women's rooms were marked with moons. This custom came from the Roman Goddess of the Moon, Diana, who wore a crescent moon in her hair. Men's rooms were marked with suns. So why not suns on outhouse doors? Maybe it's just that crescent moons are a whole lot easier to cut out than suns.

Maybe a better question is this: why are people so crazy about outhouses? Do we think outhouses are funny because we're glad we don't have to use them much? In most of North America you've usually got to go camping to find a real outhouse these days. In many other parts of the world indoor plumbing is not so common. If you ever travel to somewhere without flush toilet facilities, you might just have to try out the bare hole in a seat or bench. Remember, if someone directs you to the biffy, the backhouse, the johnny or the latrine, they're probably sending you to an outhouse.

There once was a fellow named Hyde
Who fell down a privy and died.
His unfortunate brother
Then fell down another
And now they reside side by side.

What does the nursery rhyme Ring Around the Rosie mean?

Ring-a-ring o' roses
A pocket full of posies,
A-tishoo! A-tishoo!
We all fall down.

We've all heard this rhyme. It's sung to accompany one of the most popular nursery games — join hands, dance in a circle chanting this ditty, and you all fall down at the end. But what's it really all about?

The story goes that the "ring around the rosie" is about a rosy rash, a symptom of the Great Plague of London, which devastated the population of London, England around 1665. Posies were the herbs that people carried to protect them from the plague, and sneezing was the last symptom before they fell down dead.

Well, sorry to disappoint, but the rumour spreaders are reading a little more into it than is meant to be there. There are dozens of variations on this rhyme, all as full of nonsense as this one, so to say that it has deep meaning probably isn't so. It's just a game for circling and falling down, that's all.

Interview some kids and adults, and see how many of them "always believed" that that rhyme was about the Plague. Probably most of them will have bought into that particular tale.

How did jumping rope originate?

It's an old game, perhaps even thousands of years old. There are drawings of rope makers in Egyptian tombs. They used the hemp plant, an herb with a stringy and tough stem, and twisted and twisted it to make it stronger. When people figured out how to make rope, they soon figured out that twirling a rope around and jumping over it was possible. Jumping rope was likely an adult's game at first. There is an ancient Greek statue of a maiden "skipping" with a vine rope. Then, when boys started to work at rope factories, they became the rope jumpers.

Double Dutch came along pretty early too, as it was an obvious next step. It just took two ropes being turned in two different directions. It is called different things in different places, including Double French, Double Irish, Double Orange and Double Rope.

The weird thing, from today's perspective, is that only in the last hundred years or so have girls been allowed to jump rope. It was solely a boy's game until then. Boys didn't sing at all, but did pepper, Double Dutch, and so on. Likely a big factor in letting girls play was the newer clothing designs that made moving around a lot easier. When girls started jumping rope, the boys stopped.

It was girls, though, who added all the songs. Many of them were originally clapping songs. There are some books containing these songs, but mostly jump-rope rhymes get passed on orally over the years. This is partly because little girls really get into it before they can read much, so verses are memorized and passed on by word of mouth. Ask your mother for her favourites.

Why do some people have a wake after a funeral?

Some wakes are wild, even drunken parties that usually happen after a funeral. This kind of gathering is called a "wake" because that is another form of "watch." That is what many people did when someone died — the mourners would keep watch through the night. This custom has been around for hundreds of years.

Some people think that this kind of wake is in bad taste, and disrespectful to the person who has died. Others feel that when you are sad it is good to get together with others and mourn together. You can talk about the person who died, and party to celebrate his or her life. Wakes are particularly popular in Ireland, so people often call them an "Irish Wake."

The wake may come from a medieval custom called "rousing the ghost" that had mourners partying to test if the corpse was really dead. If that sounds bizarre, it was because sometimes in the old days keeping "watch" was to make sure the body didn't get buried unless it actually was dead. Remember, there weren't scientific instruments then to test whether a person was really dead. So the party was a send-off . . . unless it happened to "wake" up the dead if they were still alive!

Why are boats and ships given female names?

Nowadays boats and ships aren't always given girls' names, but a boat or ship is mostly referred to as feminine. You always call it a "she," not a "he." That mostly dates back to ancient times. It has to do with the fact that the word for "ship" is a feminine word in most languages, like French or Latin. English nouns don't have this gender connection, but somehow Englishmen picked it up and it stuck. (Those female figureheads often seen on the prow of a ship were to frighten away evil spirits, by the way. They weren't connected to the name or gender issue.)

Naming boats has always been a bit tricky. In ancient times people believed that a name was an integral part of a ship, and if you changed that name, all sorts of nasty things might happen. The ship would be cursed. There are lots of stories about ships being lost or smashed after a name was changed. Since most ships were originally named after gods, changing the name would insult and anger that god as well as the sea gods. It is still considered to be unlucky, unless the ship's name changes when the boat's ownership changes.

The best names are easy to remember, easy to spell, easy to pronounce and mean something significant to the owners. Thirteen-letter names are unlucky, but if you can come up with a seven-letter name, you will have luck. Names with three a's are considered good, especially ones like *Niagara* or *Arcadia*, since they have seven letters and three a's.

Right now the three most popular pleasure-boat names in the U.S. are *Odyssey*, *Serenity* and

> When you are naming your boat, keep in mind that some time you might have to call for help on the radio. So if your boat is called *None of Your Business*, *Scatterbrain*, or *Hasty Banana*, you are going to sound like an idiot.

Obsession. Up there in the top ten are also *Escape, Therapy* and *Solitude.* These top names are all pretty serious. There are lots that are much sillier and more in the sport of fun and boating. *Mama's Mink, Second Mistake, Branch Office, Fuelish Pleasure, Run Aground Sue, Slippery When Wet, Tooth Ferry, Aliens Ate My Buick, This Side Down* and *Never, Never Land* are but a few.

Why do women change their last names when they get married?

In our society, names have often been the property of men because it is usually fathers who give their surnames to their children. Traditionally, boys are supposed to bring honour to that name when they become men, as girls will exchange their names for their husbands'.

This ties in to women's position historically. Through much of history, women owned nothing, and were regarded as the property of their fathers — and after they married, of their husbands. But women have often preferred to be known by their own names. Many found that being called by their husband's name and "Mrs." made them feel rather invisible. Other women didn't mind at all.

Sometimes though, the man or society made the choice. If a woman called Mary Smith married John Brown she became Mrs. John Brown. There's not much of her left in that name. Mrs. Mary Brown was an improvement, but there were times when Mrs. John Brown was the only accepted form. Some women even "took on" their husband's profession, as with Mrs. Doctor John Brown.

Early feminists paved the way for the fairly common practice today of women choosing to keep their own names. The most famous was Lucy Stone, who retained her name when she married in 1855. Feminists were working on all kinds of other issues too — education, the vote, property rights, and the right to divorce. The Lucy Stone League was founded in 1921 in North America to encourage more women to follow her example. Prominent Lucy Stoners in the 1920s included Margaret Mead, Amelia Earhart and Edna St. Vincent Millay. There were some people doing this in the 1940s, but it has only been in the past twenty years or so that the practice has become fairly common. The etiquette books reflect this too. *Emily Post* in 1922 says, "a wife always bears the name of her husband." The 1981 *The New Bride's Book of Etiquette* talks about how to keep using your own name for bank accounts and so on, if that is your choice.

The term "maiden name" is out of favour. "Birth name" or "woman's own name" is more proper. Today many women keep their names because their careers are under their own name, and it's easier for their professional lives. It used to be just movie stars who did that.

Many women have a deep emotional attachment to their names, so they don't want to take someone else's. This is totally a woman's choice, but that doesn't mean that people around her are always happy about it. Her in-laws, parents, friends and husband will have an opinion. Legally, in North America a woman has the right to change her name, and she has the right to not change her name.

Some modern women believe that even by keeping their own names they are identified with their fathers. They choose some new name of their own, usually one associated with their mothers, or some personally meaningful name.

Here's the big question: If women keep their own names, what do you name the children? Most give the father's name and more and more often the middle name is the mother's last name. Some double-barrel the two parents' names, like Jingleheimer-Schmidt. In the next generation or two it will be interesting to see what happens with children's surnames. Will names simply be added and added? How about McGillicuddy-Glockenspeil-Jingleheimer-Schmidt?

Why are valentines heart-shaped and red, and why do they symbolize love?

That heart shape? It's questionable. That shape usually seen on valentines is similar to a real heart with the twin lobes of the atria — similar but not terribly close. Some artist has definitely played with that real heart, probably in the 1400s where it shows up as one of the suits on a deck of playing cards. Desmond Morris, the famous anthropologist, thinks it looks like stylized human buttocks, which apparently have romantic connections. Some think the top of the heart looks like women's breasts and the narrow part at the bottom could be a tiny waist.

The redness of the valentine is likely associated with the colour of blood pumping through your heart. People who believe the theory that the heart is like a woman's breasts figure the red colour would have to be connected to a woman's lip colour.

A heart as the symbol for love has been around since at least the twelfth century. St. Valentine's

Day has been a celebration of love since Roman times. Back then young people would gather together and each young man would get to draw a young lady's name. This couple were "valentines" for the year, and exchanged love tokens. This custom eventually transformed into love notes and cards passed around on February 14 to mark the day. The simple illustration of a heart would be an obvious adornment for such cards and letters.

Valentine cards were available for sale as early as 1800.

Why do people get on a horse from the left side only?

They don't all the time, but most people mount from the left most of the time.

Many Western horses are trained to let you mount or dismount from either side. That's because there might be situations where you need to do that. Say you sprain your left ankle, or you are on a trail or a ridge where there is no room to mount on the left but there is room to mount on the right. It is smart to know how to mount from both sides.

Why this left/right thing? It is definitely geared toward the majority of the population who are right-handed, and it has historical roots in the military. Right-handed people are more comfortable using the right leg to swing over the horse. (Right-leggedness is the most common too).

Another reason people mount horses from the left is because soldiers carrying swords could not mount from the right. Right-handed people wear the sword on the left side of the body. If you tried to mount the horse from the right side, your sword would be in your way.

We know much about horsemanship from the peoples of the East, such as Persia in the seventh century B.C. They started the custom of the approach (by grooms) and the mount and dismount (by cavalrymen) from the left side. Mounting was done by springing onto the bare back of the horse, unless a groom or companion would give you a foot up. Another way would be to plant the butt of a javelin held in the left hand, and use the leverage on it to vault astride the horse, swinging your right leg over. Some Greek vase paintings, illustrating what appear to be riding-school lessons, demonstrate this type of mount.

A very early book on equestrian matters, written by Xenophon in the fourth century B.C., is called *On Horsemanship*. It shows clear mounting instructions, including a rider being able to mount and dismount from both sides.

Since horses get used to the one-sided mount, they tend to look upon any attempts to mount on the "wrong" side in an unfavourable manner — they buck.

Why do we eat popcorn at movies?

and Other Fascinating Facts About FOOD

Why do we eat popcorn at the movies?

Mostly because popcorn is cheap and easy to get. (Plus it's crunchy and tastes great too.) Popcorn has been around for at least 5600 years. The story goes that the chief of a New England tribe handed the Pilgrims a bag of popcorn on the first Thanksgiving Day in 1621. Of course the popcorn wasn't in the red-striped paper bag we see today; it was presented in a deerskin bag. The Pilgrims ate it the next morning for breakfast with sugar and cream — the first puffed cereal. It didn't catch on as breakfast cereal, but it has been a favourite snack food for a long time.

What's popcorn's connection to the movies? People had been eating popcorn in their homes and buying it from street vendors since Jolly Time brand popcorn showed up around 1914. When movies were first shown in the 1910s, they were usually in fancy theatres where food was not allowed. (There was no sound to the movies then, so all that crunching would be really distracting.) After the stock market crashed in 1929 these expensive theatres closed. Smaller and cheaper places opened. The theatre owners soon realized that their customers were bringing in popcorn they had bought from street vendors, so they started to sell popcorn in order to make that money themselves. Even in tough times, people usually had a nickel for a bag of popcorn. And with the coming of "talkies" — movies with sound — all the crunching was masked.

The great thing about popcorn is that it costs very little to produce and there is a high profit because there is no middleman — just buy the corn from the producer, then make and sell the final product yourself.

Nowadays theatres make most of their profit from the concession stand. This is especially true if the theatre is showing expensive first-run films. So, as well as being a treat for moviegoers, popcorn helps keep the theatres in business.

POPCORN FACTS:

- 98% of the kernels should pop. If not, the popcorn is likely stale or low quality.

- The unpopped kernels are known by lots of different names (other than "maddening" and "hard on your teeth") such as duds, spinsters, UPK's (unpopped kernels), or old maids.

- Don't keep popcorn in the fridge because it dries out.

- Not all corn pops — popcorn is a special corn whose nuggets explode when the water in them is heated and expands to steam.

- Before corn poppers were invented, popcorn was often made in a shallow cooking pot placed on the fire. Coarse sand was placed in the bottom of the pot, and the corn was mixed in. As the corn popped, it rose to the surface, leaving the sand behind.

- Popcorn is popular in theatres all over North America, but if you went to the movies in Israel you might eat sunflower seeds. In Egypt you'd get cheese on pita bread and falafels, and in Nigeria theatres sell little fried cakes with peanuts and hot pepper. No matter where you travel, you will always find Coke!

- Most theatres don't use paper bags anymore. Cardboard containers are quieter, especially for the romantic scenes. Theatres also wanted to stop kids from blowing up the paper bags and popping them!

How big a bubble can you blow with gum?

Susan Montgomery of Fresno, California blew the biggest bubble from bubble gum in 1994 — a 58.4 cm bubble. She once burst a bubble with such a loud pop someone thought it was the sound of gunfire!

What about the world's largest soap bubble? In 1995, Alan McKay of New Zealand used a bubble wand, dish detergent, glycerin and water to make a bubble 19.45 metres long.

Did Sir Isaac Newton really get hit on the head by an apple . . . and if so, what kind was it?

This is a question of utmost gravity. And it is ripe with opportunity for bad jokes. But we will get to the core of the matter.

Apples have been around for a long time. Archaeologists have found evidence of apples from 6500 B.C. and we know that the Egyptians grew apples in the thirteenth century B.C.

Over all these years, a lot of apple lore has come along. Fruit in the Garden of Eden tempted Eve, and it is assumed that the fruit was an apple. William Tell shot an apple off his son's head. Newton came up with the law of gravitation by seeing an apple fall from a tree in England in 1666. But what kind of apple?

Was it a Gravenstein (Get it: gravity)? No. Gravensteins are from Italy and came later. Was it a Newton? No. Newtons are from New Town, Long Island in the U.S., and came along in 1759.

The apple was from a tree called the Flower of Kent, a variety from around 1629. That particular tree was so famous that it was well looked after until it died in 1814. Then the wood was used for chairs.

While this famous tree was still alive, more trees were made from it by grafting parts of it onto new roots. That's called propagation. So babies of the famous Newton Flower of Kent apple tree have been planted in front of Physics labs all over the world. Those trees remind scientists that sometimes the best discoveries come from the simplest places.

Why do so many kids hate liver and Brussels sprouts?

There are four basic reasons why these two foods are different from ones that kids will eat. Liver and Brussels sprouts taste bitter, have unusual textures, and smell odd. Add to that their colour — or lack of colour, since Brussels sprouts get to be a rather pale green when cooked, and liver goes sort of grey. Yuck.

Probably the strongest reason of the four is the taste. Children's taste buds are just developing, and haven't matured enough to enjoy these two goodies. Liver actually tastes more bitter to a child's tastebuds than to an adult's.

Can you go deaf by listening to rock concerts?
and Other Weird Notes About MUSIC

48.

Why is it so easy to remember words to a song, even years after you first heard it, when it's nearly impossible to remember lines of a poem you have to recite in class, or a list of facts?

It's true, songs are relatively easy to remember. There are two main reasons for this. The first reason is the song itself. A song is often a very organized and catchy piece of work with lots of rhymes, and usually with some repetition too. The rhymes, the words and the repetition are all "cues" to help you retrieve it from your brain. Chances are that if you like a song you listen to it over and over, and this repeated listening also helps you recall it. The second reason is that music is a very emotional experience. We enjoy emotional experiences like this very much. The key here is that we remember experiences having positive emotions far more easily than traumatic or nasty experiences. (If something really nasty happens, we can have a very hard time remembering it.)

So the positive emotions, combined with a song's cues and its structure, make it much easier for us to remember words to a song, even many years later.

Try putting lists of facts, or poems that you want to remember, to a favourite tune — it can't hurt, and might help you to do a much better job of remembering.

and d... Polished up the handles of the big front door

Can you go deaf from listening to rock concerts?

One loud rock concert isn't going to damage your hearing permanently. But repeated attendance at live concerts can definitely do damage. The sensitive hair cells (cilia) in the inner ear are destroyed by repeated exposure to loud noise. Once damaged, these hair cells cannot be repaired, ever. Concerts are often as loud as 100 to 115 decibels, and the closer you are to the speakers, the louder and more damaging the sound gets. As a comparison, a single exposure to gunfire that is over 150 decibels can cause permanent damage to your hearing.

When the music is loud, you get a temporary hearing loss — things seem muffled or you have ringing in your ears — which is a warning sign. One problem with this is that people turn up the music to compensate, and make it even worse for their ears.

You don't have to go to a rock concert to encounter music this loud. School dances are often over 100 decibels. Ask to have the music turned down. It is still enjoyable and easy to hear when it is turned down. Plus, your voice won't be hoarse from yelling at your friends, which is another problem.

Try some earplugs at concerts. There are new special earplugs for musical concerts that don't change the way the music sounds, they just make it quieter.

Why can people who usually stutter manage to sing without stuttering?

A big problem for stutterers is tension in their vocal cords. Vocal cords lock up, and stuttering is one way to loosen them up. Now think about singers — their vocal cords move constantly, so they can't tense or lock up. Add that to the fact that when you sing you aren't thinking of something to say, you are singing words that you know and have memorized. And the singer can think about the music rather than just the words.

Stuttering seems to be related to a faulty link between the left side of the brain, where words are initiated, and the voice mechanism. Since music is connected to the right side of the brain, the stuttering doesn't kick in. Many stutterers also use musical tricks to avoid stuttering. Winston Churchill, the former Prime Minister of Great Britain, would hum before he made a speech, and that let him get through without stuttering.

What makes people tone deaf?

There isn't a simple answer to why some people are tone deaf. First of all, what does tone deaf mean? Basically, it means not being able to hear the highness or lowness of a note of music, so it is impossible to sing it on pitch.

Pitch means how high or how low a note is. Think of a piano — each key is a different pitch. Sometimes you don't hit the note right on pitch when you are singing — you fall between the keys.

You can be sharp or flat because your aim is off or your sound production is bad.

Tone is the quality or resonance of your pitch. So if you're tone deaf you don't hear where the note is supposed to go. You don't hear the C or whatever note you're aiming for — so you can't match the pitch because you can't perceive the difference.

If someone is missing the pitch, they can be trained to produce better quality sound and to hit the note they're aiming for. But it doesn't work if they can't perceive the sound. These folks are tone deaf and aren't physically able to do it. The worst part is that they think they are singing on pitch because they can't hear themselves singing flat or sharp, so it can be awful for anyone listening.

Tips for better tone:

- If you don't want to wreck your voice, don't whisper or yell.
- Don't drink really cold water because it shocks your voice muscles.
- Milk can encourage some people's bodies to make phlegm, which interferes with the clarity of their voice.

Why do my parents usually hate the music I like (and vice versa)?

Hate might be a bit strong — parents often just aren't into what you like. You have probably suspected this all along.

Research shows that people tend to get more and more stuck in their ways as they get older. It has been proven that as people head toward middle age, they become considerably less interested in trying new experiences. Pair that with teenagers often wanting the latest — in music, fashion and food — plus the fact that they often rebel against their parents at this age, no wonder there is often conflict.

Kids are usually more physical than adults too, and like to feel the vibrations and literally be moved by their music. (You have to be careful, though. The amplifiers can make a person physically sick.) Most adults prefer to be touched by music in other ways — in their hearts, their minds or their spirit, rather by being more physically "moved" by the noise.

Why are people so terrified of giving a speech?
and Other Unusual ODDS AND ENDS

Why are people so terrified of giving a speech?

Because it is scary stuff. Fear of public speaking is a real biggie — many people's number-one fear. Standing in front of a crowd is scarier for these people than the fear of death and disease, or even the fear of falling off a cliff. Why? Because it's performance, and the accompanying anxiety is totally normal.

Think of the last time you gave a speech. Were you trembling or sweating, did you have clammy hands, was your heart racing, your tummy queasy, your voice shaking? Were you blushing, a bit confused, losing your train of thought? All of these are symptoms of performance anxiety. It might be a fear of failure, a fear of making a fool of yourself, or just a general fear. If you can lick this, though, you can do almost anything.

The crowd doesn't have to be an auditorium full of people. You might get scared doing an oral presentation in front of your class. The good news is that you can get over performance anxiety . . . but it will take awhile. First you have to stop avoiding speaking in public. Then try some small things to get you more comfortable. Try asking a few questions in class. Read out loud at the dinner table in front of guests. Contribute to a group discussion or do a little presentation somewhere. Ask for some help from your teacher or your parents. These coaches will remind you to relax, help you to structure your ideas, to rehearse, and to breathe! Being well prepared and calm is the key to feeling confident enough to soar through a performance.

What did we use before toilet paper?

The oldsters always refer to using pages from a Sears Roebuck or Eaton's catalogue, or pages from old books or newspapers — but that was after paper and printing was cheap. What about before that, or for folks who didn't read? Corncobs. Yes, the cob that corn comes on. Eat the corn and you have a cob that could be dried and hung in an outhouse to be used for cleaning up. Throw it down the hole and it would compost nicely. (This makes catalogue pages seem very hygienic and convenient, not to mention soft!) And when you are camping, leaves seem to be the t.p. of choice. Just be sure to avoid stinging nettles.

In some countries people use nothing but water to clean themselves after going to the bathroom. The left hand is always used for cleaning. That's why in India you must only use your right hand for eating. To do otherwise would be gross and very impolite.

Why are so many cars black, red, white, blue or grey?

When Henry Ford built the first Model T in 1908, he told customers that they could have it in any colour, as long as it was black. Things have progressed since then, and today there are dozens of choices. Colours change with fashion too. Blue and grey were once very popular with fleets like delivery cars and rentals. Red and white were the most popular for private buyers.

Recently dark green has been hot, rivalling white, which had been the long-time favourite (especially in warm climates since it doesn't absorb much heat, and it looks clean and simple). White is still the lead colour for luxury cars, and trucks and vans. More natural colours like tan, and light greens like sea foam, are apparently coming into popularity. Aqua, silver and purple are moving up too.

People like a change, and colours have cycles of popularity. The DuPont Corporation, a huge supplier of automotive paints, does a lot of research on colour preferences so that car designers and stylists can try to predict what colours will be most popular in the future.

Sixty per cent of men and fifty-one per cent of women aged eighteen to thirty-four say that colour is an important factor in their car purchasing decision.

56. Why is a car's performance measured in horsepower?

James Watt, a Scottish engineer, invented the steam engine. Because horses had been the main method of power before his invention, he came up with the idea of horsepower to compare the power of his engine to the power of horses. Watt was trying to establish the rate of doing work. He figured out how much coal a horse could haul in a minute, by what he called a foot-pound (how much work it took to move one pound the distance of one foot). He worked out that one horsepower is 33,000 foot-pounds of work per minute, or 746 watts.

So what did that mean? Mostly it meant that a standard for comparison had been established. When the steam engine gave way to car engines and electric motors and other powerful devices, there was a way to compare them. A car engine's horsepower lets you know how powerful your car is — how fast it will go from 0 to 100 kilometres per hour. Modern cars go up to 200 horsepower.

Why do golfers yell fore (or is it four?) when teeing off?

This is a warning: you are forewarned. (That is a hint.) You wouldn't want a golf ball to whack you when a golfer hits it with a huge amount of force. So golfers yell "Fore!" to warn you that it is coming.

Golf has been around since the fifteenth century, and something has been yelled in warning ever since. "Fore!" is likely a shortened form of the military phrase, "Ware before!" (from "Beware"), which was used to mean "Look out ahead!" or "Duck!" because guns were going to be fired over your head.

What does the post office do with all the letters addressed to Santa Claus, and why did kids start writing to him in the first place?

Canada Post gets just under one million letters to Santa a year, because everyone knows that Santa lives at the North Pole, which is in Canada. Kids from all over the world write to Santa Claus, North Pole, Canada HOH OHO. All across the country, Santa has hundreds of helpers. Every letter is answered. Volunteers, mostly retired postal workers, are the ones who actually reply to the children's letters. If a letter is in another language, it goes to Ottawa, where there are translators for about twenty languages.

There are helper letter-from-Santa writers in other countries too. In the United States, many of the children's letters are sent to Santa Claus, Indiana, and returned with the town's postmark.

The most famous Santa letter was written in 1897 by eight-year-old Virginia O'Hanlon of New York City. She wrote to the editor of the *New York Sun*.

Dear Editor,

I am eight years old. Some of my little friends say there is no Santa Claus. Papa says, "If you see it in *The Sun,* it's so." Please tell me the truth, is there a Santa Claus?

Virginia O'Hanlon

And this was part of editor Francis Pharcellus Church's response:

Yes, Virginia, there is a Santa Claus. He exists as certainly as love and generosity and devotion exist, and you know that they abound and give to your life its highest beauty and joy. Alas! How dreary would be the world if there were no Santa Claus! It would be as dreary as if there were no Virginias. There would be no childlike faith then, no poetry, no romance to make tolerable this existence. We should have no enjoyment, except in sense and sight. The external light with which childhood fills the world would be extinguished.

Not believe in Santa Claus! You might as well not believe in fairies. You might get your papa to hire men to watch in all the chimneys on Christmas Eve to catch Santa Claus, but even if you did not see Santa Claus coming down, what would that prove? Nobody sees Santa Claus, but that is no sign that there is no Santa Claus. The most real things in the world are those that neither children nor men can see. Did you ever see fairies dancing on the lawn? Of course not, but that's no proof that they are not there. Nobody can conceive or imagine all the wonders there are unseen and unseeable in the world.

Why *do* people close their eyes when they kiss?

and Other Mysteries About THE OPPOSITE SEX

Why do people close their eyes when they kiss?

Why not? When you think about it, kissing is so weird anyway, smashing lips together. Why not noses or forearms or ears? Most people do close their eyes when they kiss. It is sort of a reaction to the nice, comfortable warmness of the moment. And you don't want to be distracted.

But there is a more practical reason. You can't really keep your eyes open and look at your partner without going cross-eyed. The trick is to close your eyes right after you lock lips because if you do it before you might mash noses. Done right, kissing is lovely, but it isn't worth worrying about the eyes closed/open thing. It will just come naturally.

By the way, the kiss as a romantic act is fairly recent. It only dates back to medieval times.

Some kissing superstitions:

- If your nose itches, a fool will kiss you.
- If you are kissed by a chimney sweep, you'll have good luck.
- Sneeze on Tuesday, you'll kiss a stranger.
- Kiss a deck of cards before you play and you'll win.
- Kiss over a gate, you'll have bad luck.

Why do girls get taller before boys?

Girls start earlier for sure. Girls get a growth spurt when they are around ten and a half, while boys take until twelve or thirteen to get growing. So if you look at a grade six or seven class picture the students are all different sizes — they don't grow evenly. The girls are often ahead of the boys, but the girls don't all start at the same time, either, and of course they will end up different heights.

Whenever your body gets around to making these changes, that time is called puberty.

And that growth spurt in puberty is because of rising levels of hormones called androgens. Both boys and girls have androgens, as these hormones come from the ovaries, testes and adrenal glands. Androgens make your bones grow, and your shoulders broaden. Androgen levels start to rise in girls before they do in boys, and that's why girls start their growth spurt before boys.

Estrogens, another type of hormones, also influence how much bones will grow, in both boys and girls. Girls' bodies make more estrogens than boys' do, and when estrogen levels get high enough, bones stop growing, so girls usually don't grow as big as boys. Estrogens also cause fat to be added on girls' breasts and hips.

None of these changes hurt much — they are all natural — but you will find you need lots more sleep to let your body do its thing.

Why do boy babies get dressed in blue, and girls in pink?

Long ago, many people believed that evil spirits hung around the nursery, but that these spirits were repelled by certain colours. The most potent colour was blue, associated with the heavenly sky. Blue was believed to frighten away demons and rob them of their power. So blue on a baby was not only adornment, but also seen as a very necessary precaution.

Now this was a long time ago, when girls were considered inferior, so boys got the really potent blue colour — it didn't matter what colour girls got. The assumption is that later generations chose pink for girls to symbolize that new rosy all-over-pink look.

Why can't you tickle yourself?

and Other Strange Stories from SCIENCE

Why is so hard to get rid of hiccups?

Hiccuping (or hiccoughing — that's a clue) is a funny and rather rude reflex action, sort of like coughing or sneezing or even vomiting. Maybe you ate or drank too fast, and swallowed some air. It might be a stomach problem and you need to get rid of some gas. It might be that you have a tickly throat, or maybe the nerves that control your diaphragm are a bit jumpy. Whenever one of these things happens you can react with a hiccup.

Most people hiccup for a minute or two. It can be somewhat annoying, but is usually quite funny. Sometimes, though, people can't stop. One man in Iowa started hiccupping in 1922 and stopped in 1990. That's sixty-eight years! In the meantime he got married twice, had eight children, and led a normal life. Obviously he even figured out how to sleep.

If you are just a regular hiccupper, a loud "Boo!" can often make you stop. It'll scare the extra breath out of you. What happens is that the shock of the scare distracts your nervous system and it "forgets" to hiccup. If you sneeze, the same thing can happen. But getting yourself to sneeze is pretty hard. You can gargle, tug on your tongue, or try drinking water upside down. But mostly, when your hiccups want to stop, they will . . . hopefully before sixty-eight years have gone by!

Why do we get electric shocks in our fillings when we chew on aluminum foil?

Whoa, this makes my teeth hurt just thinking about it. It is a shocking experience indeed when your filling — which is made of an amalgam (a mixture) of silver or tin and mercury — touches aluminum foil. Suddenly you get an electric reaction. That's because when you put two different kinds of metals together, in the right circumstances, you can get a quick zap of electricity.

A man named Count Volta discovered this in Italy in 1800. That's where we get the word "volt" from — it is a measurement of electrical current. Count Volta stacked up a tall pile of discs: copper, cardboard soaked in salt water, zinc, then copper, soaked cardboard,zinc, etc. again. Then at the exact same time he touched the top and bottom discs on the stack and got a shock. What he had created was, in fact, the first battery, but at the time they called it a voltaic pile.

In your mouth the aluminum foil and your filling are the two metals. Then your saliva works like the salt water, which is needed for the charge. Contact is made when you bite, and a small current gets going, which the nerves in the teeth can feel. That's how you get the shock.

Why do WintO Green Lifesavers spark in the dark?

Try this yourself. Stand in the dark in front of a mirror. Put a WintO Green Lifesaver in your mouth. (It has to be a fresh one; if it is soggy you get no sparks.) Crunch down hard on the Lifesaver and bingo — sparks! Bluish sparks will burst from your mouth. It's a fabulous sweet spark. Tiny but impressive.

Why does this happen? It's called *triboluminescence*. That's what happens when crystals fracture. *Triboluminescence* is the light that is the result of crystals crushing or tearing.

Here's what happens.

Everything around us is made up of atoms like carbon, nitrogen, hydrogen and oxygen. The atoms are made up of tiny particles — electrons, protons and neutrons. Atoms cluster together in groups called molecules. When you crunch the sugar crystals in a Lifesaver, electrons break loose and zip around. Invisible nitrogen molecules that are in the air can detect an opening where the electrons have broken free, and zoom into that spot. All this happens very fast. The electrons that broke off the sugar crystals in the first place decide they want to return to the fold, but since the nitrogen molecules are already there, the electrons crash into the nitrogen. They re-combine with a bang. And that crashing together results in light — in fact, in ultraviolet radiation. It's totally safe; you can't get a sunburn from this tiny spark. But it is impressive.

Add the fact that this ultraviolet radiation has hit the wintergreen flavouring (which is called methyl salicylate) and you get the bluish tinge to the glow. You can actually get almost all crystal sugar candy to give you a bit of light when it is crushed. This was first noticed in Italy in the seventeenth century. But for most crystal candy it is a rather dim light. It takes wintergreen to really light up your life.

It's probably much more scientific than you need to know — but now you do. The important thing is that it's fun. And it is a good party trick too — just don't break your teeth!

How are marbles made?

Perfectly spherical marbles are really pretty things. They are favourites of collectors, and have been toys for thousands of years. Archaeologists have even found clay marbles in the pyramids of Egypt. Marbles are called marbles, by the way, because in the early seventeenth century they were made of marble, ground into spheres. There were also aggies made of agate, and commies (for common-ies) made of inexpensive clay. But now marbles are mostly made of glass.

Marbles are either made by machine or by hand, worked off spun-glass rods. The glassmakers heat the rods until the glass is molten and then cut it and round it off. In the middle of the nineteenth century a German glassworker invented marble scissors that made mass manufacturing of marbles a possibility. These scissors were a simple cupped tool that rounded a hot glass marble in one step, instead of having to round them by hand. You would form the shape by pressing the hot end of the glass into the cup of the marble scissors, and turning it several times. The scissors were then pressed together and twisted slowly until the rounded glass was separated from the glass cane.

65.

Then the slightly hardened marbles were rolled in a wooden barrel where they gradually cooled and become more round.

Today most marbles are made by machine. Glass (which is made of sand, soda ash and lime) is melted at between 1300 and 1400 degrees Celsius for up to twenty-eight hours, until it is the consistency of molasses. This batter is poured, cut and put through rollers, then cooled and made into little balls. It's a bit like cookie dough — but a lot hotter.

Different technologies have made it possible to make different kinds of marbles: clearies or purees, which are one clear colour; various coloured and patterned swirls; corkscrews in various colours; bumblebees (black and yellow); and Vaseline glass that is fluorescent in colour. In the 1950s the Japanese came up with cat's-eye marbles that are clear, except for a vein of brightly coloured glass. How do you get those sparkling swirls or spirals in marbles? You take a striped glass rod and twist and twist it, and then shape it as usual.

**For more info check out this Web site:
The Marble Collector's Corner at
http://www.blocksite.com/**

How was duct tape invented?

You know what is said about duct tape: You only need two things in life: WD–40 to make things go, and duct tape to make them stop.

Duct tape is the handyman's secret weapon. Need to fix your canoe, your car or your sneakers? There are thousands of uses for this great, sticky grey tape.

Duct tape was invented during World War II to meet an important need. At that time, it was called "duck" tape. The American armed forces needed a strong, waterproof mending material that could be ripped by hand to make quick repairs to Jeeps, aircraft and other military equipment. There was also a need for something to keep moisture out of ammunition boxes.

Johnson & Johnson were already producing adhesive tapes for medical uses, so they just added a rubberized waterproof coating. Waterproof, like a duck . . . and *voilà* — duck tape.

After the war there was a housing boom in the United States. Many of the new homes had fancy new heating and air-conditioning units with ductwork. The military tape was perfect for binding and repairing these ducts. The tape began to be produced with the rubberized topcoat in a sheet-metal grey colour (so it would blend in with the ducts) and duct tape was born.

This handyman's secret weapon is no longer a secret. There are entire books devoted to describing zillions of uses for duct tape, there are jokes about duct tape, and even world wide web home pages about it. In fact, the WWW is where these words of wisdom were found: "Duct tape is like the force,

light on one side, dark on the other. It holds the
universe together, and if not handled properly,
becomes a sticky mess."

**If you need to know more about duct tape, there's even a Web site:
http://paul.spu.edu/~miostiek/ducttape/ducttape.html**

67.

How are hurricanes named?

A hurricane or a typhoon is actually a strong
tropical cyclone. That's a huge storm with very
heavy winds — winds, in fact, that are higher than
119 kilometres per hour, often with large amounts
of rainfall. Less than 119 kilometers per hour is
called a tropical storm. For a hurricane to get
started the ocean-water temperature has to be over
26 degrees Celsius. That means these storms
usually come in the late summer and early fall in
the tropics. Hurricanes can also start tornadoes,
and the wild winds and rain can cause huge
increases in sea levels, and flooding too.

The quiet centre of a hurricane, called the eye,
shows up on satellite images. It can be 16 to 48
kilometres wide. But surrounding the peaceful part
are wild winds at speeds up to almost 300
kilometres per hour. To whirl the core of the winds
that fast takes 500 trillion horsepower! That's the

equivalent of exploding an atomic bomb every ten seconds.

Before this century, hurricanes were named after the saint's day on which the hurricane appeared. Now, an alphabetical list of twenty-one names is made up by the World Meteorological Organization in Geneva, Switzerland. Since 1971 the names have alternated in gender from male to female, and skipped the letters Q,U,X,Y and Z because there aren't many names that start with those letters. The people who make these decisions choose names for the remaining twenty-one letters, names that are distinctive, not too long, and easy to pronounce and remember. The names on the North American list are also international — English, French or Spanish — because those are the three languages most used in North America.

The further along in the alphabet a hurricane name comes, the more hurricanes there have been that year. For example, in 1996 there were hurricanes called Opal and Pablo — it was a bad year. If the list only gets to Gordon, like in 1994, there weren't many hurricanes.

When there is a really fierce hurricane which is highly destructive and costly, the name will be retired for at least ten years. So far almost forty names have been retired, names like Anita (1977, Mexico), Cleo (1964, Lesser Antilles, Cuba, southeast Florida), Gilbert (1988, Lesser Antilles, Jamaica, Yucatan Peninsula, Mexico) and Hugo (1989, Antilles, South Carolina).

This chart from the World Meteorological Organization shows the current six-year rotation of names for hurricanes or tropical cyclones in North America. The list recycles every six years.

1998	1999	2000	2001	2002	2003
ALEX	ARLENE	ALBERTO	ALLISON	ARTHUR	ANA
BONNIE	BRET	BERYL	BARRY	BERTHA	BILL
CHARLEY	CINDY	CHRIS	CHANTAL	CRISTOBAL	CLAUDETTE
DANIELLE	DENNIS	DEBBY	DEAN	DOLLY	DANNY
EARL	EMILY	ERNESTO	ERIN	EDOUARD	ERIKA
FRANCES	FLOYD	FLORENCE	FELIX	FAY	FABIAN
GEORGES	GERT	GORDON	GABRIELLE	GUSTAV	GRACE
HERMINE	HARVEY	HELENE	HUMBERTO	HORTENSE	HENRI
IVAN	IRENE	ISAAC	IRIS	ISIDORE	ISABEL
JEANNE	JOSÉ	JOYCE	JERRY	JOSEPHINE	JUAN
KARL	KATRINA	KEITH	KAREN	KYLE	KATE
LISA	LENNY	LESLIE	LORENZO	LILI	LARRY
MITCH	MARIA	MICHAEL	MICHELLE	MARCO	MINDY
NICOLE	NATE	NADINE	NOEL	NANA	NICOLAS
OTTO	OPHELIA	OSCAR	OLGA	OMAR	ODETTE
PAULA	PHILIPPE	PATTY	PABLO	PALOMA	PETER
RICHARD	RITA	RAFAEL	REBEKAH	RENÉ	ROSE
SHARY	STAN	SANDY	SEBASTIEN	SALLY	SAM
TOMÁS	TAMMY	TONY	TANYA	TEDDY	TERESA
VIRGINIE	VINCE	VALERIE	VAN	VICKY	VICTOR
WALTER	WILMA	WILLIAM	WENDY	WILFRED	WANDA

Do astronauts use a key to start the space shuttle?

Like a key to start a car or a snowmobile? No, at least not the sort you might put on a key ring or hang around your neck. Space Shuttles are entirely controlled by a computer. The reason a key isn't used is that the computer has to time the launch events really carefully. It has to be incredibly precise, as exact as thousandths of a second. Keys and humans just aren't precise enough.

The launch countdown starts forty-three hours before the launch. There are hundreds of things to do to get ready: checking the software, checking the propellant line systems (which carry the fuel that gets the rocket going), loading the liquid hydrogen and liquid oxygen into the external tank. Then the crew needs to get on board.

At T – 9 minutes (T minus nine, or nine minutes to take-off) the computer, called a ground launch sequencer, takes over. Then at T – 26 seconds the ground-support equipment gives control of the orbiter to the four on-board computers that control the order of the launch. The computer on the ground and the computer onboard the Shuttle talk to each other and cooperate in opening and closing valves, turning on and off switches, and ensuring that take-off happens on time, to the fraction of a second. The pilot and commander just watch all the data.

Some ferries, which hold 500 cars and 2000 people and are the length of 2 football fields, have 4 engines that are 500 horsepower each. A computer controls the start-up of these ferries, just like on the Shuttle.

Why can't you tickle yourself?

Have you tried? It just doesn't work. Tickling is all about surprise, and about losing control. When someone tickles you, you spend most of your time giggling and trying to get away at the same time. There is a bit of danger there — someone is attacking you, but your brain figures out that it is just in fun, so you start giggling. The reason you can't tickle yourself is because there is no "danger" and no surprise — so no giggling. It's just the way it is.

Do animals dream?
and Other Fascinating Facts About SLEEP

Do animals dream?

It seems that they do. Watch your dog or cat sometime, and you can tell it is dreaming of running after something. Its eyes twitch, sometimes it moves its paws — something is happening in its dreams. Scientists think that most warm-blooded animals dream. They have monitored goats, sheep, cats, dogs, rats, mice, monkeys and apes, and all had dream periods and symptoms — except the spiny anteater, which seems to be a dream-free mammal. Probably the animal that spends most time dreaming is the opossum.

Hunting animals like cats, dogs and humans spend more time dreaming than animals that are hunted, such as cattle, rabbits, sheep and goats.

What is the crust in your eyes when you wake up?

Sleepies, and you have to rub it out! Some people call it sandman dust, sleepy seeds or eye gunk. It usually shows up on the little circular bump at the corners of your eyes, near your nose.

Your eyes have a lot of glands that make tears. When the tears have flowed over your eyes they drain near that bump in the corner (called a *commissure*) and go into your nose. Then you swallow them away.

At night when your eyes are closed, the tears slow down to almost nothing, but what tears there are roll down to the corner expecting to drain out. Since your eyes are closed, the drain is closed too, and the tears, along with a bit of oil and sweat, make up the crust. Crusty, but no big deal.

Why do you drool when you nap?

Not everyone does this. It is fairly rare, and far from a desperate medical problem. We are constantly moving our tongues and circulating our saliva, and in our sleep we usually also swallow our saliva. But when some people are sleeping lightly, like during a nap, the saliva doesn't get swallowed. It is also possible that their heads are on a funny angle for napping, such as on the couch, so swallowing, which is an involuntary action, doesn't happen. Nappers get a low quality sleep and a low quantity of sleep, and the drooling is proof that it is only a nap.

Why do people snore?

The noise that drives you bananas when your brother snores is the sound of air rushing through narrow air passages in his throat and nose. It vibrates against his tonsils, tongue or the soft tissue of his palate, or roof of the mouth.

This sound can get really loud, even louder than ninety decibels, which is defined as as the highest amount of sound you can stand in the workplace. But lots of us do it: thirty to forty per cent of adults are snorers. Men snore more than women — half of men do. The worst culprits are overweight middle-aged men. Only around thirty per cent of women snore, and even then they don't snore all the time.

If you sleep by yourself, snoring is no big deal. But couples sharing a bed, or siblings sharing a room, can have really bad nights (and bad fights) if one is a snorer. You have heard people call one another "mouth breathers," meaning stupid. Snorers are serious mouth breathers, but there are some ways to make them stop. If you can get snorers to change position, often you can stop the snoring, but that means you have to wake them up enough to get them to turn. People who sleep on their backs snore the most, so some books suggest tying tennis balls to the back of their pajamas so they can't sleep on their backs.

If snorers would lose weight that would help. So would avoiding alcohol at bedtime, since it clogs up your nose. Quitting smoking would help too. Sometimes snoring is a result of allergies, a broken nose, or a bigger than normal tongue, adenoids or tonsils.

There are a number of wacky looking appliances on the market to try, which all hold the jaw and/or tongue forward to keep the airway open. Ow! It hurts even thinking about it. Snorers can also try laser surgery, but that sounds extreme. The other solution? Whoever has to sleep with a snorer can buy a large box of good earplugs.

Do bedtime tricks or routines help people sleep better?

Some people just go to the bathroom, brush their teeth and hit the hay. They fall right to sleep and that is that. But there are many who need to do certain things in a certain order to make themselves calm enough to get a good night's sleep. Some people need a snack, a warm bath, a good read . . . and maybe then they can get to sleep.

You need to sleep so that your body can rest, build up energy and stay healthy. People who don't sleep well get sick more easily; disease usually attacks the tired and weak. If you are ten to twelve years old you need about eight or nine hours of sleep every night. Researchers say that teenagers really need to sleep in, and that they don't do well in the morning. Tell your parents or your school that!

There are some tricks to getting a good night's sleep. Stay away from scary books or movies or TV shows before bedtime. You'll be riled up and you might get nightmares. Try not to do anything too frantic, like wrestling, but if you can do something that really tires you out, like swimming, you will be much happier. Hot baths are great for calming down. Some people like to write in a journal before bed, or write a list of everything that is bugging them before they sleep, so they won't be bothered by those thoughts all night long. Reading before bed is a nice ritual that can make you sleepy.

Of course there are bedtime and sleep superstitions too. Some people say you need to watch which way your head points. North means you will have short days, south means you will have a long life. If you want to be rich, point your head east, and if you want to travel, point west. Whatever it takes, just do it, because you always feel so much better after a good night's sleep.

When we are younger we all sleep on our belly or side much more, and as we get older we are all more likely to sleep on our backs. The most common sleeping position for women is on their back. For men it is on their belly or their side.

Is it true that if you didn't have dreams you would go crazy?

No one knows if this is true, because everyone dreams. We all dream every night, usually four to six dreams for every night's sleep. People who think they don't dream have actually forgotten their dreams. We know all of this because of studies in sleep laboratories.

Dreams are wild things. There are thousands of people involved in the industry of interpreting your dreams — academics, therapists and hobbyists. There are dream encyclopedias and dream dictionaries to tell you what the meaning of your dream supposedly is.

There are loads of superstitions involved too. Before analysts like Sigmund Freud and Carl Jung got into the act, people believed that dreams were your connection to the supernatural world, and could foretell the future. In some cultures it is believed that you dream because your soul leaves your body during sleep and goes out wandering.

There are many superstitions about dreams:

- Dreaming the same dream three nights in a row means that it will come true.

- You will have good luck if you forget your dream from last night. You can't tell your dream until after breakfast or it won't come true.

- If you have a dream on a Friday night and talk about it on Saturday it will come true for sure.

- In some cultures, whatever you dream, the opposite will come true. Dream of a funeral, for example, and a new baby will show up.

- To dream of the future, some people sleep with a key or a horseshoe under the pillow.

- If you go to a wedding and sleep with a piece of wedding cake under your pillow, you will dream of the person you will marry.

Sleep Facts:

Some animals sleep a lot in twenty-four hours!

Little brown bat: twenty hours

Giant armadillo: eighteen hours

Squirrel: sixteen hours

Cat: thirteen hours

Dog: twelve hours

Guppy: six hours

Horse: three hours

Tortoise: less than one hour

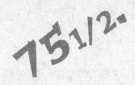
75 1/2.

Why do horses sleep standing up?

There wouldn't be any room in the bed if they all slept lying down.

What does a horse do all those hours if it only sleeps for three? Grazing animals can spend up to eight hours a day in a sort of dozing state. They're not active, but they're aware enough to know if there's any danger, and can rouse in time to escape from a predator. Horses actually lock their legs so they can sleep standing up, but giraffes have to lie down to sleep.

Who invented the wave?
and Other Winning Facts About SPORTS

Who invented "the wave" in baseball, and where was it first performed?

Who? Well, two guys claim this fame, both believing they invented it in 1981. The more famous is "Krazy George" Henderson, a professional cheerleader with serious lungs who madly bangs a drum and can be quite obnoxious to opposing teams. He was at the Oakland Coliseum cheering an American League playoff game between the Oakland A's and the New York Yankees. George had an idea. He ran from section to section getting the fans to stand up, yell and sit down again quickly. Then the fans did it again and again, faster and faster. It was the start of something big. And something funny.

But a band director at the University of Washington claims he started the wave that same fall. Bill Bissell was at a Huskies football game, and led a cheer with a former student and cheerleader, Robb Weller, then co-host of *Entertainment Tonight*. They got different dorms and fraternities and sororities to stand up and sit down, and to do it faster and faster.

Krazy George usually gets the credit for the wave, and he still cheers for a living. You can watch for him on TV. The wave is now done all around the world, and at other sports like soccer and basketball.

What's the history of the seventh-inning stretch?

There are lots of ideas about the origin of the seventh-inning stretch, some more believable and more fun than others. Probably the best story is that in 1910 U.S. President William Howard Taft, a big fan of baseball, was at the season's opening game. He got up from his seat at the start of the seventh inning, and the whole crowd figured he was leaving, so got up to salute the president. And that turned into a tradition — the seventh-inning stretch.

Why is tennis scoring so weird?

Tennis seems so simple — you hit a ball over a net, you hit it back. But the scoring isn't so simple. You don't get a point when you score — you get fifteen. Add the fact that tennis players start throwing around the words deuce and love and it can be quite confusing.

The scoring system comes from using the four quarter-hours of a clock (15–30–45–60). At 60 the game would be over, while 45 was eventually cut down to 40. No one really knows why "love" is used for a score of zero, but some think it comes from the French term *l'oeuf* for egg — a big zero. Or maybe it is from the notion that doing something for love is like doing something for nothing (zero). So if you keep playing and keep getting zero, you must really love the game.

Where did the idea of cheerleaders come from?

Minnesota, or so the story goes. In 1898 the Gophers, the University of Minnesota's football team, were having an unbelievably lousy year.

The Gophers were in last place, the coach was hopeless and the fans were lifeless — mostly because cheering wasn't a natural thing then. Cheering was a half-hearted "The team's all right" sort of call when there was a goal — but there weren't many of those. So the crowd just sat there, making the team feel even worse. Someone wrote a letter to the paper to encourage fans to yell, but it didn't really help.

One young man, a first-year medical student, decided to lead the yells, and that was the beginning of cheerleading in the United States. Soon someone figured out that applauding individual plays, not just yelling randomly, was a good idea. Students starting thinking up songs and appointing "yell captains." Words were added to old tunes like "Hello My Baby" and "There is a Tavern in the Town." It all worked. The Gophers played better and better, and word started spreading to other college teams. By 1900 cheerleaders and a group of 200 young men who called themselves the Rooter's Club started using megaphones.

There was no turning back. Parades were added before games, as was blowing a whistle every time the team scored, and having a victory parade after every win. Eventually cheerleading for professional sports moved on to the women's domain. Short skirts and pompoms followed. But guys still do cheers on college campuses, as loudly as ever.

Why are hot dogs so popular at baseball games?

Long before there were hot dogs in the United States, German butchers developed sausage making. Frankfurters were developed in Frankfurt, Germany, and wieners in Vienna, Austria. German immigrants brought the franks to America along with sausages. But it wasn't until 1900 that hot dogs came to be sold at baseball games. One cold day a man running the concession was having no luck with ice cream or soda, so he went out and got some "red-hot dachshund sausages," and the fans loved them.

One day a few years later, Tad Dorgan, a newspaper cartoonist who was watching a ball game, made a drawing of a real dachshund, smeared with mustard and stuffed into a bun. He couldn't spell dachshund, so he labelled the picture "Get your hot dogs." The name was so perfect that hardly anyone calls it a frankfurter or a wiener anymore.

Some people say "hot dog!" to exclaim that they are excited about something. "Hot diggity dog!" is an even bigger exclamation. Since America came up with the term "hot dog," the world thinks it is an American invention. It is certainly one of the most popular foods in the United States, especially at baseball games!

What do athletes do to bring good luck to their game?

Many, many things. Things you can't imagine that grown men and women would do. And they believe strongly in these superstitions and amulets or lucky charms, so strongly that some of them wouldn't play the game if they couldn't do the rituals they think bring them luck, or if they didn't carry their lucky charm or amulet.

Lucky numbers:

- Say you have a big success as number 7 on a team. You are going to want to be number 7 as often as possible — it is your lucky number for that sport. Another popular lucky number is 13.

- Some football players figure that double numbers on their uniforms (like 44) will bring good luck. They also think it's bad luck if a player takes a new number when he's traded to another team.

- Numbers aren't restricted to jerseys. Some golfers believe that you need to start your game with odd-numbered clubs. And they think they will have bad luck if they play with balls with a number higher than 4.

Lucky food:

- Some athletes have to eat the same meal before each game, like pasta or pancakes or maybe steak. Usually it is the same meal they ate right before they had a big win.

Lucky clothes:

- Michael Jordan, who doesn't really seem like someone who needs luck, since he is such a good athlete, wears lucky shorts. He puts on University of North Carolina gym shorts under his uniform because in 1982 he was part of the winning team in the NCAA basketball championship.

- Olympic swimmer Tom Dolan has to wear his black basketball sneakers to every meet. That started in his first year at the University of Michigan. The whole team wore those sneakers, and won nine meets that year.

- Many bowlers believe that they should wear the same clothes to keep a winning streak going.

- Tennis players don't like to wear yellow clothes because they believe the colour will give them bad luck.

Necessary routines:

- Hockey star Eric Lindros is a neat freak. He likes things in his dressing stall just so. That is part of his routine before a game. His sticks have to be taped in the same way each time, and he eats the same meal of pasta and chicken before each game. He also has a two-hour nap before playing.

- Mo Vaughn of the Boston Red Sox has a routine for dressing. He does it left to right: first the left sock, then the right; first the left pant leg, then the right.

- During games there are routines too. Many basketball players believe they must bounce the ball before taking a foul shot for good luck.

- Hockey players like to tap the goalie on the shin pads before a game.
- Baseball players like to spit into their hand before they pick up the bat — not to get a better grip, but to bring good luck!

Cowboy Superstitions

To have good luck:

- Saddle bronc riders always put the right foot in the stirrup first.
- Cowgirls often wear different coloured socks on each foot.
- Some cowboys eat a hot dog before a rodeo competition.

What can bring bad luck:

- Never kick a paper cup thrown down at a rodeo.
- Don't compete with change in your pocket because that's all you might win.
- Never put your hat on a bed or wear yellow.

Why is scoring three goals called a "hat trick" in hockey?

It certainly has nothing to do with pulling a rabbit out of a hat. And it has nothing to do with what was called a hat trick in the British House of Commons about a hundred years ago. (A member would save a seat for himself by putting his hat on it.) This hat trick is for a player scoring three goals in one game. But it is not orignally a hockey term, nor is it originally Canadian.

"Hat trick" comes from the game of cricket about a century ago. A cricket bowler who got rid of three batsmen on three balls in a row would have a new hat bought for him by his teammates. By 1909 this term came into general use in many sports to celebrate a three-fold feat. And hockey picked it up early on in the game.

Why is 13 considered unlucky?

and Other Strange SUPERSTITIONS

Why is 13 considered unlucky?

The number 13 has been considered unlucky for a long time, and by people all over the world. The early Romans thought 13 was a sign of death and destruction. And according to Norse mythology, if you sat 13 people down at a table, that was very unlucky. (Why? At a banquet of 12 people in Valhalla, an intruder — number 13 — caused the death of Balder's son Odin.) The number of people at the last supper of Christ and the twelve Apostles confirmed the superstition about the number 13 in Christian countries. And in the Middle Ages witches were believed to meet in "covens" that had 13 members.

The fear of the number 13 is called triskaidekaphobia. Many hotels have no room 13, and many buildings have no 13th floor. Next time you fly, see if there is a row 13 on the plane. As a date, 13 isn't too lucky either, especially when it falls on a Friday. That was always thought of as a really bad day to start a new project or to begin a ship voyage. Movers, doctors and dentists say their business drops on Friday the 13th. The good news is that a maximum of three Friday the 13ths can occur in a year, and sometimes there is just one.

Good facts associated with the number 13:

- Richard Wagner liked the number 13 because he was born in 1813 and composed 13 operas.
- Theatrical producer Florenz Ziegfeld preferred to sail and open his shows on the 13th.

- U.S. president Woodrow Wilson once had 13 guests to dinner. This was met with a lot of protest by his guests, but he declared the number to be lucky.

- According to one Texas superstition, a bag filled with 13 sow bugs tied around a child's neck will cure the child of thrush, or sores in the mouth.

Bad facts associated with the number 13, Friday and Friday the 13th:

- French Lick Springs, Indiana, once passed a law requiring all black cats to wear bells on Friday the 13th.

- Some Texans say never to cut any kind of garment on Friday, because it will never be completed.

- Greek philosophers called 13 an "imperfect" number.

- Friday was a common day for people to be hanged. Thirteen pence halfpenny was at one time the wage paid to the hangman.

Mr. Smarty Pants, *The Austin Chronicle*

Why are black cats considered unlucky?

The Egyptians of 5000 years ago actually considered cats very important and lucky. They were the first to believe that cats had nine lives. It was against the law to hurt or kill a cat, and when a cat eventually died it was embalmed, wrapped in linen and put in a mummy case made of bronze or wood. Because wood was expensive and rare then, we know that this custom was really important, and therefore that cats were considered important. All cats were treated this way — black cats included. Archaeologists have even found entire cat cemeteries.

In later centuries leaders in India and prophets in China kept cats. Until about 500 years ago cats were not considered unlucky, but some people began to become suspicious about how independent, strong and stealthy cats were. (There was also the problem of huge population increases, since spaying and neutering weren't done.)

Then there was an uproar over the possibility of witches in Europe. Many people thought a lot of the old ladies were doing black magic, and that their black cats were witches too. In fact, black cats at night were thought to be human witches during the day. It doesn't make a lot of sense now, but in those times the rumours flew.

Strange as it may seem, the cat that had been revered by ancient people was now considered evil. So evil that, until King Louis XIII stopped the practice in the 1630s, thousands of black cats in France were being killed because people were so afraid of them.

Some people still think it's unlucky to have a black cat cross your path, but after Louis XIII's pronouncement black cats started to be connected with a few good luck omens too:

☙ You can stroke a black cat and wish on it for luck. Sometimes sports teams keep one for luck.

☙ A visit from a black cat is supposed to bring you luck, but don't shoo it away or you will get bad luck.

85.

Why does a horseshoe bring good luck?

There are lots of reasons horseshoes are considered lucky, but here's a good one: There was a blacksmith called St. Dunstan. One day into his shop walked the devil, Satan, wanting shoes for his cloven hooves. St. Dunstan knew it was the devil, and convinced him that in order to have the shoes attached, he had to be shackled to the wall. The devil bought this, and St. Dunstan did a nasty job of putting on the shoes, hurting the devil really badly. Then he said he would only let the devil go if he would never enter a Christian's house again. The devil, in desperation, agreed, but wondered how he would know which houses were Christians'. St. Dunstan thought quickly and said that the sign would be a horseshoe over the front door. That's why it is good luck — it keeps the devil out.

More lucky horseshoe lore:

A horseshoe is also shaped like a crescent moon, is made from iron (which has magical powers), and usually has seven (a magical number) nail holes. To be really lucky, the horseshoe must be real, and a used one is better than new. If it comes from the near hind leg of a grey mare you are really in luck. If you find it on the road — bingo! You have to pick it up, spit on it, and make a wish at the same time. Then you throw it over your shoulder, or nail it outside over the door to your house. You get extra luck if you use its own nails to nail it to the house, and if there is an odd number of nails. To bring good luck to the house, the points have to go up, so the luck won't "run out."

Why do people throw salt over their shoulder after spilling some?

Salt has always been a symbol of life. We know now that it is necessary to preserve the proper chemical balance in our bodies. In the past, people knew salt was an excellent antiseptic for wounds, plus a flavouring and a preservative for all kinds of foods. Without salt, we couldn't live. Salt was so important that it was once used as money, even as a sacrifice to the gods.

Salt has also come to represent good — some people refer to a good person as "the salt of the earth." That's why if you spill this "good" thing, it is bad luck.

What can you do to stop the devil from undermining your life if you spill salt? The devil is supposed to lurk over your left (or sinister) shoulder, so you toss salt over your left shoulder and hit the devil in the eye. He hates salt.

This salt over the shoulder custom has been going on for thousands of years. The ancient Sumerians chucked salt. The Egyptians, the Assyrians and the Greeks did it. And it shows up in the Leonardo da Vinci painting of the last supper. There, Judas spilled the table salt, indicating that there was about to be a tragedy — his betrayal of Jesus.

Why does a bird in the house mean a death is likely to occur?

It is mostly because a bird is thought to be the returned soul of the dead. Since the beginning of time, birds have had all sorts of superstitions associated with them. But this is the most famous: if a bird flies in through an open window it means the death of someone who is in that house. It is widely believed that a person's soul will go out with the bird.

Why were twins considered so unlucky that in ancient times the second twin might be left to die?

We know now that identical twins are the result of the mother's fertilized egg splitting, so that two babies are formed instead of one. (With fraternal twins, two eggs are actually fertilized.) But people in ancient times figured that if there were two children there must have been two fathers, which was a sin, or that God or some spiritual being had been involved. They were highly suspicious of twins, so they did what they thought was right. They got rid of one or both of the babies, and usually punished the mother.

But different societies through the centuries have viewed twins differently. The ancient Egyptians were keen on twins. They actually worshipped twins called Osiris and Set. Ancient Romans were keen on twins, too. They had twin gods, Romulus and Remus. These twins were the offspring of a god and a mortal. The ruler of the day wanted them drowned because they were the grandsons of his rival. Their basket was left on the edge of the flooding Tiber River, and was found by a female wolf who nursed the twins until a king's herdsman found them. He and his wife raised the boys. Eventually word got out who they really were. Remus got into crime and Romulus reluctantly had to kill his brother. Romulus went on to be the founder of Rome.

A number of North American tribes had twins as gods. On Canada's west coast the Tsimshian believed that the wind was the "breath of twins." And the Kwakiutl believed that twins could influence the weather and help the fishermen.

More recently, the fate of conjoined twins has been followed closely. These types of twins, which are extremely rare, are physically bonded through a malformation of a part of their body. The most famous pair was Chang and Eng, born in Siam (hence the old name, Siamese twins) in 1811. They were ordered by the King of Siam to be put to death when they were thirteen years old because the king believed they must be evil. Fortunately, a British merchant rescued them. They went on to work at a circus sideshow and then retire as farmers in North Carolina. Chang and Eng married sisters and had a total of twenty-two children between them. They died in 1874 within two hours of each other.

Many people believe that twins are special. Some twins can sense how their other twin is feeling through some sort of telepathic bond, even if they are far apart. Maybe twins always have someone to talk to — psychically, or in person.

Superstitions about having twins:

- If a husband spills pepper, he has to throw some of it over his left shoulder or his wife will have twins.

- If a pregnant woman eats twin fruit (two pieces of fruit that have grown together), she will have twins.

Why is it bad luck to open your umbrella indoors?

The word umbrella comes from the Latin word for shade, *umbra*. But where do umbrella superstitions come from? Egypt for starters. The Egyptians used umbrellas to shade themselves from the sun. Umbrellas were considered to be status symbols and religious objects. That's because Egyptians believed that the sky was in fact the body of the goddess Nut. Her toes and fingertips attached to the earth as she arched her body over it, sort of like a big umbrella. When you carried an umbrella, the shade it made was said to be special. Bad luck occurred when someone stepped into the shade created by your umbrella.

The umbrella came to England from Italy, where it was used to keep out sun and rain. The bad luck associated with opening an umbrella *indoors* comes from London, England, in the eighteenth century. Why bad luck? For starters, it was dangerous to open an umbrella indoors. Umbrellas were awkward, with their stiff spokes and nasty points, and if someone knocked over a lamp or candle (remember, this was before electricity) they could cause big trouble.

Opening an umbrella *indoors* was also thought to be dangerous because an umbrella was an *outdoor* thing, so it went against doing things "the right way" — the way people thought God intended.

They also believed that if you opened up your umbrella inside, it would rain outside, and you didn't want that. We still have a goofy belief that if we take our umbrellas to school or work, it won't rain, and if we leave them at home it might rain.

What are the real rules on breaking apart a wishbone for good luck?

The wishbone is the forked bone overlying the breastbone of most birds. It is the most prominent bone, and easiest to retrieve from a chicken or turkey. It is called a wishbone because of the superstition that when two people pull the bone apart a wish will be fulfilled for the person who gets the longer piece. Actually, a wishbone is a charm, like a horseshoe or a four-leaf clover. These are all objects you can make a wish on.

How? With a wishbone you have to dry it first for a few days — three is a good magical number — until it is brittle. Then two people (usually children) pull it apart by hooking their pinky fingers around the ends. The person who gets the longer piece will have his or her wish come true. Sometimes it takes some measuring, but there will always be a longer side. In some families it is said that the wish will only come true if it is not revealed to anyone. (The same belief holds for wishing on the first star each night, and the wish made before blowing out birthday candles.)

Before 400 B.C. the Etruscans killed a sacred fowl known as a "hen oracle." They dried the collarbone, and the person looking for an answer from the gods made a wish on this "wishbone" by stroking it and making a wish.

In the British Isles a wishbone was sometimes called the merrythought, as in, make a merry wish. Back in the seventeenth century a person would put a wishbone on the nose like a pair of spectacles. Then he would think his thought or make his wish and shake his head until he shook the wishbone off his nose. Then it was pulled apart, and the winner would get his or her wish.

Things then got even more complicated: the winner would put both parts into his hand and the other person would draw. The one who drew the long part got his wish, the other didn't.

It is said that wishbones were snapped at the first Thanksgiving in the United States in 1621. So an ancient Etruscan superstition has come a long way.

> Whoever wins the wishbone pull definitely gets "a lucky break," which is where that expression comes from.

Why aren't you supposed to walk under ladders?

The obvious reason is that you might get hit on the head by the tools of some carpenter or painter who is up on the ladder. But the historical reason isn't so obvious. If you lean a ladder up against a wall you get a triangle — and that three-sided form is thought of as representing the trinity of the gods. If you walk through the triangle you break the Holy Trinity, putting you in league with the devil instead.

The Egyptians thought the ladder was good luck. It could be used to climb to heaven. But later, when Jesus Christ was crucified, his followers decided the ladder was bad luck because there had been a ladder resting against the crucifix to take him down from it. Now ladders meant wickedness and death and betrayal, so you didn't want to walk under one.

So what should you do if you walk under a ladder by mistake? You could make the "fig" sign. Thrust your closed fist, with the thumb sticking out between the index and middle fingers, at the ladder to wipe out the bad luck. You could also spit through the ladder, spit over your left shoulder, cross two fingers and keep them crossed until you see a dog, or don't speak until you see a four-legged animal.

> When criminals in France and England in the 1600s walked to the gallows to be hanged they were made to walk under a ladder — as if they didn't already have enough bad luck.
> With those odd origins, the superstition began to take on lots of meanings: Do it and you will be hanged, or do it and you won't get married that year — a dangerous situation for a marriageable woman in times when single women were vulnerable or scorned.

92. Why do kids save their baby teeth for the tooth fairy?

Why would the tooth fairy want all those teeth? What could she do with them? There are lots of ideas. Maybe she makes a necklace and wears it to the Dentists' Ball.

Let's think about it. The custom is really about an exchange: money for used teeth. That's a fair exchange, so this shows it's good magic, not evil.

We may not believe this today, but for thousands of years people did. Any body bits — whether hair or nail clippings or teeth — that were discarded by people were magically linked to their owners. Even if you could hide these lost body parts, they were still part of the owner, because someone could take that bit of you, do some magic thing with it, and hurt you. Like grinding up your tooth to give you a toothache.

In Germany there is a folk belief that says any new growth in your teeth will be like the teeth of whatever creature took away the lost tooth. So a rat or a mouse or even a beaver is most welcome to spirit away your tooth, because they have very tough teeth.

In England and North America children usually put their teeth under a pillow or a mat, or in an eggcup, on a clock or in a glass of water. The teeth are exchanged for a coin.

Why does the tooth fairy want the teeth?

Here are some more theories:

- The tooth fairy saves your teeth and gives them to new babies — that's how babies get teeth.

- The tooth fairy puts the shiny teeth up in the sky and that's how stars get made.

- The tooth fairy puts a magic spell on the tooth and turns it into a dime — that's where coins come from.

- The tooth fairy uses them to build her castle and her village.

Who started chain letters anyway? And why are people afraid to break the chain?

Chain letters must originally have been somebody's idea of fun. They started just before the 1920s when people sent postcards with chain prayers. Then came postcards that said something like "Good luck, copy this out in the next twenty-four hours and send it to nine people. Do not break the chain or you will have bad luck — count nine days and you will have great luck." The threats of terrible tragedies for breaking the chain started to become more outrageous, and the whole idea began to lose its innocent flavour.

Then another kind of chain letter surfaced, offering big material returns for not much effort. You got a letter that had a list of a certain number of people. You were supposed to send something. Most often it was money, but sometimes books or pretty underwear — whatever the letter told you — to the person at the top of the list. Then you dropped off their name, (which moved the second name to the top) and added your name to the bottom of the list. You sent out this letter to the specified number of people, and eventually you would receive lots of items or money in return. The instructions usually included some sort of guilt factor, because if you broke the chain you would never get any money or books — nor would anyone else.

If everyone followed through, you could potentially get a lot of stuff. This results from what is called a geometrical progression, and this assumes that no one breaks the chain. If you sent the letter to ten people this is what could happen:

Level one (You are #10 on the list)

People involved: 1

Level two (You are #9 on the list)

People involved: 10

Level three (You are #8 on the list)

People involved: 100

Level four (You are #7 on the list)

People involved: 1000

Level five (You are #6 on the list)

People involved: 10,000

Level six (You are #5 on the list)

People involved: 100,000

Level seven (You are #4 on the list)

People involved: 1,000,000

Level eight (You are #3 on the list)

People involved: 10,000,000

Level nine (You are # 2 on the list)

People involved: 100,000,000

Level ten (You are #1 on the list)

People involved: 1,000,000,000

So say you sent $10.00 to the person at the top of the list. When you got to #1 you would get 10 x $1,000,000,000 or $10,000,000,000 ($10 billion).

Sound too good to be true? Well, it is. The first chain letter asking for money appeared in Denver in 1935. Each person was to send in a dime, and the big payout would be $1562.50. It made the Post Office a madhouse — one day they had to deal with 285,000 letters by hiring dozens of new staff. The Post Office decided that chain letters were illegal.

And there are other problems. There is the fact

that people break the chains. Even worse, look
at the final numbers. It would take years for the
population to expand enough for there to be
enough people to support the payout to you.

Another problem is that the chain letter is a
classic example of a "pyramid scheme." It is
gambling, it is a bad investment, and it is illegal in
most places, mostly because somebody always loses
— usually the people at the bottom of the list. So
there is absolutely no good use for chain letters. If
you want to get mail, write some letters. Your
friends will respond, eventually.

Why does February have fewer days?

and Other Tantalizing Facts About TIME

Why is Newfoundland time half an hour earlier than the Maritimes? How do time zones work?

People playing Trivial Pursuit often argue about the number of time zones Canada has. (Mostly because people can't figure out if it is six or seven.) Trivial Pursuit is a Canadian invention, and so are time zones. Sir Sandford Fleming is widely credited with creating them, but why did he need to come up with a system at all?

For thousands of years time was purely a local concern because people didn't travel much and they certainly couldn't get anywhere fast. Sunrise and sunset set up the boundaries of the day, and the church bell might indicate other significant hours. As the pace of life picked up so did the use of clocks and watches, but time was still a local thing.

Then the steam-powered ship came along, as well as the train. The world was shrinking and all of the unco-ordinated times started to be both annoying and terribly confusing. The timetables were crazy.

When the United States finished its cross-continental railway in 1869 the confusion got worse. And in Canada there were five local times between Halifax and Toronto, rather than a single one-hour shift, as there is today. At the same time there was a revolution in communication. Telephones didn't exist yet, but there was a telegraph system. People needed some sort of solution, an east–west "measurement" around the world.

Although the equator, the longest line of latitude, which divides the globe into northern and southern hemispheres, was an obvious choice as the prime parallel for latitude, no one meridian for longitude was uniquely qualified as prime. Until a single prime meridian could be agreed upon, each nation was free to choose its own, with the result that nineteenth century maps of the world lacked a standardized grid.

All sorts of people offered ideas. The navigators and astronomers and meteorologists had been complaining for years about inconsistencies with time in different locations, but now company presidents and politicians were in on it. Time was beginning to mean money.

An American, Charles Ferdinand Dowd, was trying to get the American railways to recognize uniform zones in the U.S., but it was Fleming, a Canadian, who pushed for the international view. He suggested dividing the world into twenty-four time zones of fifteen degrees each, starting it from a prime meridian drawn through the Pacific Ocean at some point that avoided land. This process took a while, but finally in 1884 the International Prime Meridian Conference decided to go with the Greenwich line as the prime meridian. It passes through London's Greenwich Observatory; where a metallic marker indicates its exact location. (The prime time zone actually extends 7.5 degrees to each side of the prime meridian.)

Each degree of latitude and longitude is divided into sixty minutes, and each minute divided into sixty seconds, making it possible to assign a precise numerical location to any place on earth.

There are twenty-four standard time zones, each consisting of a one hour segment. The day begins at midnight GMT or Greenwich Mean Time. Now it is called UT or Universal Time.

So what about Canada? If you look at a map, for each fifteen degrees of longitude there is one time zone, more or less. (Times zones tend to follow political boundaries, so that a whole province or country can share the same time zone.) Starting from the west we have Pacific, Mountain, Central, Eastern, Atlantic and Newfoundland time zones. But that's only six. There used to be a seventh. Until 1973 the Yukon shared a time zone with Alaska; now it is part of Pacific. (Trivial Pursuit has it wrong.)

And what about Newfoundland? The half-hour difference was decided upon in 1884 when Newfoundland was not part of Canada. Local mean time of St. John's was three hours and thirty minutes west of Greenwich, England (as opposed to Halifax being four hours from Greenwich) so that's why it is always half an hour earlier in Newfoundland than in the Maritimes.

95. How did February come to be the month with two (or three) fewer days than the other months?

Basically, some month had to take the short straw. Why? Mostly because of math and the moon. This started in the eighth century B.C. when the Roman calendar was figured out. Until then there were only ten months — no January or February at all.

According to some historians, it was Numa Pompilius, a Roman king, who decided to make a change and add 2 months. He worked the year out to 355 days (12 lunar cycles), which was close. The Romans were superstitious about even numbers, though, believing that these numbers were bad luck, so the Roman calendar had only 29– or 31–day months. To arrive at 355 days there had to be one shorter month, and February was chosen. March was the beginning of the year then, so February was the last month and in the dead of winter. Maybe the Romans also figured that if one month had to have some bad luck attached to it because of the even number of days, it might as well be a short month.

Julius Caesar gave the calendar another once-over much later, and bumped the total up to 365 days. He kept February short because it was a month that no one really liked. His calendar is called the Julian calendar, and was used until 1582. Then Pope Gregory XIII worked out his version, the Gregorian calendar, which is the one we use today.

A calendar year is exactly 365 days, 5 hours, 48 minutes, 46 seconds, so an extra day was added every fourth year to account for those extra hours. That's when we get a leap year, when the year is exactly divisible by 4. The date February 29 is added to make up the total number of days that are required over 4 years.

If people live near the International Date Line, do they get to celebrate their birthdays two days in a row?

The International Date Line isn't straight, but it is more or less along the 180th meridian, in the middle of the Pacific Ocean. Cross that line and you must change the date by one day. The key: it is one day later east of the line than west of the line.

If you are travelling west, say from Vancouver to Tokyo, your day gets one hour shorter for every fifteen degrees of longitude. When you get to the International Date Line though, you have to change the date a whole day ahead. That's because even though you're west of North America, the date line is east of Greenwich, England, the starting meridian for time. Too bad if it's your birthday, you've missed out.

What if you go the other way? If you start in Japan or New Zealand or Australia and head back to North America, you would be in luck and get two days of celebration. You get to repeat a day at the International Date Line.

To really stretch things out, you could stand on the little island of Taveuni in Fiji, where there's a signpost saying International Date Line, and step from east to west. Only problem is, it might be difficult to arrange for all your friends to get there for the party, and there aren't many locals! Not so great for a birthday party.

The exception to the leap-year rule
is that there is a leap year in
a centenary year only if it is
divisible by 400.
So 1900 had no February 29,
but 2000 does.

Is the Red Sea really red?
and Other Weird but USEFUL INFORMATION

Is it possible to dye your hair with Kool-Aid?

It is, but we don't recommend it, because the stuff will stain everything. Your bathtub could stay Purplesaurus Rex for weeks. People who have used Kool-Aid say their hair stays a good strong colour for only one to three days, then it will be a faded version of that colour for about a week. (The good thing is that their parents probably got over it sooner than if they used real hair dye.) You absolutely have to use the unsweetened stuff. Pre-sweetened Kool-Aid makes a huge sticky mess.

Kool-Aid works best on light hair — the blonder the better. If a dark brunette put Great Bluedini Kool-Aid on his hair it would look like his hair was growing mould — an icky, dull green mould.

People who have dyed their hair with Kool-Aid say you need about three packets for short hair. They dump the Kool-Aid into a small bowl or dish — glass is best as it won't stain the way plastic will — and add a tiny amount of water to make a paste (sort of thick, like tomato paste). The true colour won't be obvious at this point. Then they slap the paste all over their hair and try to comb it in until their hair dries. It is hard and clumpy and messy, even with a large-toothed comb. They leave the Kool-Aid on all day for intense colour, but some people say it works even if you leave it for just an hour or two. Then they wash the paste out of their hair . . . and start scrubbing out the shower after they rinse out the paste. Stain City!

Remember, it's not recommended that you actually try it on your hair, but it can work on other stuff. You might try dyeing some wool yarn. Mohair works best. Wash it in Ivory Liquid first so the dye will take or set better. Pour hot water (enough to cover the wool) into a container, then mix in the Kool-Aid powder. The more packages, the stronger the colour. For example, add a small amount of wet yarn to one packet of cherry Kool-Aid mixed with a few cups of water in a glass mason jar (uncovered). Zap it in the microwave for just a couple of minutes — don't boil it! Leave it in the microwave until it cools down, and the yarn will be a fabulous intense red. It smells great too — just like cherries.

A Nebraska salesman invented Kool-Aid in 1927. He hated selling soft-drink syrup in bottles; the bottles were heavy and kept breaking. So he eliminated the water, got rid of the bottles, and sold the drink powder in handy little envelopes. He called his new product Kool-Aid. At first, there were just a few flavours — grape, lemon-lime, cherry, orange, raspberry and strawberry. Now there are dozens of flavours with wacky names like Man-o-Mangoberry and Stompin-Strawberry-Kiwi.

Some people use Jell-O to dye their hair too, but it has sugar in it as well as gelatin. Talk about messy — this stuff is unbelievable. But they can really sculpt their hair with Jell-O if that's the look they're aiming for.

Why did people create money?

Money didn't have to be in the form of the coins and bills we use today, but something was needed to exchange for goods and services. It could have been chickens — but that would be a bit messy. Bricks are too heavy, and feathers would fly away. Get it? Money is really an idea or concept, more than an object.

The first humans didn't need money, but as the population increased there was a need for more food. Families would travel to hunt and gather food. They began trading with other families — maybe skins for meat or fish for shells, whatever they had for whatever they needed. They would trade goods for goods, which is called bartering.

But things started getting complicated. What if you needed food but the farmer who grew the food didn't need what you produced? That's when people started using objects as money. It could be anything as long as people agreed on its value. Salt was used as money in many parts of the world because it was valuable for flavouring and preserving foods. Shells, tobacco, blankets, tea and barley were also used, in different places. They can be a little hard to transport though — they get heavy. And salt can melt in the rain. There was definitely a need for something else.

Almost 4000 years before Christ, the Sumerians thought something needed to be done, so they started using silver bars as money. As trade started to spread around the world, ideas were exchanged as well as goods. People liked the metal money that the Sumerians had invented, so most countries began to use silver.

Coins came next. They were easy to use, and could be stamped with pictures of the country's leaders. Coins came in all sorts of metals — copper, bronze, silver and gold. In 1295 Marco Polo came back to Italy from a trip to China with the discovery that the Chinese had been using paper money for hundreds of years. But it took a long time for Europeans to catch on to paper money. Coins felt safer because the metal would always have value. Sometimes citizens didn't really trust the governments who printed the paper money.

In the colonies of North America, settlers used coins as well as things like corn and fish and wampum (belts or bracelets and necklaces made of shells, used originally by the native peoples). Mints were eventually built to produce the coins or bills we use as money, and there has been no turning back.

Now many people use debit or cash cards for money. When a debit card is used to pay for goods, the amount of money is immediately transferred out of the purchaser's bank account. Cash cards (which are called smart cards in some places) can be "filled" from someone's bank account, then used until the cash value is used up (like phone cards), and then "refilled." Debit cards, and sometimes cash cards, are even being used for parking meters and movie tickets, so people need actual cash less often. So, who knows just how long the Sumerians' invention will stick around in the future?

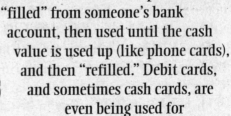

Why do drivers in some countries drive on the left, and others on the right?

Road rules are a mishmash all over the world, except on the ocean where one rule rules: ships of all sizes keep to the right (starboard side, green light), and traffic passes on the left (port side, red light). The saying goes: "Green to green or red to red. Perfect safety, go ahead." Too bad it isn't so simple on roads. It totally depends where you are whether you drive on the left or the right.

It all started back in the old days, when travellers had to worry about being attacked on their journeys. Since most human beings are right-handed (only ten per cent are left-handed), they wanted to walk on the left in order to pass oncoming people on their right, because they carried their swords in their right hands. That way they were always at the ready to do battle. Think of a knight on a horse with his lance in his hand — he kept to the left too. This was only a custom to begin with, but it was made official in 1300 by Pope Boniface VIII, who wanted no fighting among the pilgrims on their walk to Rome during that year of jubilee celebrations. He said to keep to the left, and people stuck with this ruling in Britain when they began driving.

When settlers first came to the United States they also drove wagons on the left, because that had been the custom in Europe. Some people think they eventually switched over to rebel against the Old World customs, but the truth is a better story.

It's actually about how covered wagons, called "prairie schooners" or Conestoga wagons, work.

There was no front seat, so the driver controlled the horse or oxen team by sitting on the left rear animal. That was the best position for a right-handed person to handle a whip. When two wagons approached each other, they would veer to the right, so each driver could clearly see the passing wagon's wheel hub, and avoid collision. In 1792 a law was passed confirming the stick-to-the-right custom. A hundred years later, automobiles were invented, and the steering wheel was placed on the left, the same side used by Conestoga wagon drivers.

It was the same in France. Freight wagons there were similar to the Conestogas, and also drove on the right. In Britain, however, the wagons had a driver's seat in front of the load, and drivers sat on the right side, just where the British now mount their steering wheels.

Because Canada is a Commonwealth country, most people drove on the left until the 1920s. The last place to make the switch was Newfoundland, which changed over at midnight on January 2, 1947, two years before joining Confederation. One reason Canada switched is obvious — it is so close to the United States that it would be confusing to switch sides of the road at the border.

How many countries are on each side? Of 221 countries in the world, 58 drive on the left and 163 on the right; 82 per cent of the vehicles on the road drive on the right, and 18 per cent on the left.

Exactly what is El Niño?

It's a warm ocean current, and boy can it mess up the world's weather. El Niño is Spanish for Christ Child. Fishermen along the coasts of Peru and Equador came up with the name because often the current starts around Christmas time. El Niños show up every two to seven years and will last twelve to eighteen months. They aren't a new thing — they have been documented for about three centuries, and likely happened for centuries before that. But it was only about thirty years ago that scientists started figuring out that El Niño might be responsible for some of the awful things happening all over the world: severe droughts, huge floods, hurricanes, forest fires, typhoons, torrential rains, and freak snowstorms (in usually warm places).

Scientists watch the currents with satellites, and by putting out floating buoys which measure temperature, currents and winds around the equator. The data are transmitted electronically from the buoys to researchers and forecasters around the world. Scientists are now looking back over the world's history and trying to figure out El Niño's place in it. They are even thinking that the crop failures of 1787–1788 in France, possibly caused by El Niño, might have contributed to the flour shortage that ignited the French Revolution.

For a huge resource of information try The El Niño Theme Page:
http://www.pmel.noaa.gov/toga-tao/el-nino/home.html

What did people use before toothbrushes and toothpaste?

The first toothbrush was a twig, likely a licorice root, about the size of a pencil. One end of the stick was frayed to make it soft and fibrous; it would be rubbed against the teeth.

In some places, chew sticks are still used. Some African tribes fray twigs from the *Salvadore persica* or "toothbrush tree." The American Dental Association has discovered some remote areas of the U.S. south where twig brushes, mostly from white elm, are used. Twig brushes can work as well as our nylon toothbrushes.

The first bristle brush like the ones we use today came from China in 1498. It was made of hand-plucked bristles from the backs of the necks of hogs, fastened into handles of bamboo or bone. The Europeans went in more for horsehair toothbrushes. Dr. Pierre Fauchard, who is considered the father of modern dentistry, said in his 1723 textbook that horsehair brushes were too soft. He figured a better way was to rub teeth and gums vigorously with some natural sponge.

After Louis Pasteur, a nineteenth-century scientist, proved that animal-hair toothbrushes could be a breeding ground for bacteria and fungus, people looked for an alternative. When the DuPont company created the nylon bristle toothbrush in 1938, there was no turning back.

As long as 4000 years ago a sort of toothpaste was used. In 2000 B.C. doctors made a paste of powdered pumice stone and strong wine vinegar. It must have smelled very strong, and it was very

> Picks have been popular since the Roman times. Quills could be used, or special brass or silver toothpicks made.

abrasive too. People would brush it on with a chew stick.

Perhaps the strangest "toothpaste" used was urine. The early Romans used human urine because they thought it would whiten teeth and fix them more firmly in the sockets. And it gets worse. Upper-class Roman women would pay big bucks for Portuguese urine that was said to be the strongest on the continent. Urine continued to be an active component in toothpastes and mouthwashes into the eighteenth century. It was actually the ammonia molecules in urine that did the cleaning. When people figured this out, ammonia was used instead of urine.

Artificially whitening teeth is a big business today and it has been since the fourteenth century. A barber-surgeon would file the teeth with a coarse metal tool, then dab them with *aquafortis*, a solution of highly corrosive nitric acid. The teeth looked great for awhile, but the acid eventually destroyed the enamel, and by mid-life people's teeth would be a decayed mess. Vanity rules though — these acid treatments were done until the eighteenth century!

People who performed "dentistry" were jacks of all trades. You could get your hair cut, your teeth extracted, your beard trimmed and your blood let all at the same time and place.

Toothpaste today contains fluoride that helps protect teeth against cavities. The abrasive is often silica that polishes and cleans the teeth. Glycerine is used to keep the paste creamy and prevent it from hardening. Then there is a bit of an artificial sweetener, a colourant, and flavouring like mint or wintergreen. If you don't like all these ingredients, try some baking soda with a little cinnamon added for flavour. It's simple and does a good job.

How big does a hill have to be before it becomes a mountain?

You would think that there should be a simple answer to this. There is sort of a simple answer. Hills are less than 305 metres above the surrounding area, and have to have a distinct summit or point. But they are not just small mountains. It has to do with how hills were formed.

A hill has to be constructed from loads of built-up rock or sand that has been put there over the years by glaciers and wind. Or a hill can be a big raised bump in the earth that has then worn down.

A mountain, though, has steep slopes, and sharp or rounded peaks or ridges. And mountains often have more than one climate zone, which means that plant life that grows at one altitude won't grow at the next.

Mountains form in lots of ways. Some are volcanoes, which means that after each eruption more layers of hard lava build the mountain. Some have been created because of folding and uplifting of the earth over the past millions of years. The Rocky Mountains stopped uplifting about 70 million years ago.

So it is possible to have a hill that is higher than a mountain — it depends how it was formed. But after 305 metres, it is called a mountain no matter how it was formed.

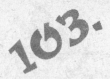

Are the Yellow, Red and Black Seas actually yellow, red and black?

Actually, two out of three are true to colour. The Yellow Sea between mainland China and Korea is yellow because of a yellow silt deposited by the Yellow River. The Red Sea, which separates northeastern Africa from the Arabian Peninsula, is red because of reddish seaweed in the water. The Black Sea (inland, between Europe and Asia) is quite dark in colour, but it is called that because it is really a stormy place with a dark and nasty character.

> The Dead Sea isn't a sea at all, but a lake filled with so much salt that almost nothing can live there.

What's the difference between a sea and an ocean?

It is an understandable confusion. We go on an ocean liner and eat seafood. Sea horses live in the ocean. We go to the seashore, and it might be the Pacific or Atlantic Ocean.

For starters, how many oceans are there? Turns out that that is a trick question. One answer could be that there is only one ocean, a huge thing that covers seventy-two per cent of the earth's surface and surrounds all of the land masses on the planet. But although there is one great ocean, called the "world ocean" or the "global ocean," the other answer is that it's usually divided into four parts or four oceans: the Pacific, the Atlantic, the Indian, and the Arctic — although some geographers disagree and call the last one the Arctic Sea. (What about the Antarctic Ocean? It's not officially an ocean, but an extension of the southern part of the Pacific, Atlantic and Indian Oceans.) When you think about it, splitting up the ocean makes navigating and describing where you are going a lot easier.

So what's the difference between an ocean and a sea? It's another trick. The dictionary will say that the words are interchangeable. The encyclopedia says that too. Geography books make it even more complicated, so let's straighten this out.

There are four major oceans, and within those are smaller bodies of water called seas. In the big oceans, the major seas are the Caribbean and the Mediterranean, which are part of the Atlantic. The Bering and the South China Sea are in the Pacific.

So sea and ocean are sort of interchangeable, but you'll do better if you use the right term for the right body of water.

Which ocean is biggest? The Pacific, by far. It holds forty-six per cent of the earth's water and it covers more area than all of the land on the planet put together.

What's a snowdome?

Those marvellous scenes in a dome, that you turn over and shake to make it snow merrily inside, are called snowdomes. They can also be called waterdomes, snowstorms, water globes, shake'em-ups, waterballs, snowscenes or blizzard weights.

The first snowdomes showed up at the Paris Universal Exposition in 1878. French glass artisans made paperweights of hollow balls filled with water and white powder. The first scene inside the dome was added in France too. A ceramic Eiffel Tower on a little square base was shown at the 1889 Exposition. *Voilà, un souvenir.* Within years, lovely blown-glass globes were being made in Bavaria in Germany, plus Czechoslovakia, Austria and Poland. These were a big hit in Victorian England, often showing scenes from fairy tales. Dome-mania made it to North America in the 1920s, mostly via Germany. The globes sat on cobalt-blue bases hand-inscribed with the names of local towns. First produced in Pennsylvania in 1927, these globes showed up in mail-order catalogues as a "new and clever novelty." Within a year the Japanese copied the Pennsylvanian designs, and the globes were everywhere. Round, square, squat, tall, with bases made of everything imaginable and encasing every scene imaginable. In 1950, when plastics became popular, oval-shaped domes were developed. Soon domes started to be made in Hong Kong, and their prices plummetted.

Thousands of serious snowdome collectors focus on all sorts of themes. Some concentrate on World's Fair domes (widely available since the 1939 New

York World's Fair), hand-blown domes only, cartoon figures, presidents, cities, countries, Christmas or religious themes, globes with moving bits inside. The very collectable are the domes that contain bloopers or mistakes, just as "blooper" stamps or coins are rare and valuable. Watch for scenes with bald bathing beauties, or Eiffel Towers labelled Puerto Rico.

How Do You Make a Snowdome?

1.

Find a dome. The easiest way is to keep an eye out at junk stores for those horrible big globes with plastic flowers (and usually rusty water) inside. Gut this dome and start again. Or check out garage sales and junk shops for flat-bottomed globes. Take them apart and clean them.

You can also use jars with flat screw-on lids, which you will use as the base for making the scene. Baby food jars are good for tiny domes. Or use any other glass dome-like vessel with a flat base that you can glue together. Some craft stores sell snowdome kits (a globe and a base) for a few dollars.

2.

Make a scene. Decide whether the snowdome will be viewed from all sides, or will have a background and foreground. Then fool around with placing figures, scenery and background. Collect bits made of plastic, ceramic, enamelled metal or glass — something that won't deteriorate in the water. Keep your eyes open. Junk stores have toys and figurines, miniature stores are great sources of materials, and railway model shops have bits of thin plastic scenery you can use. Polymer modelling clay like Fimo brand is available in bright colours too. You can create people and props to scale, then bake them.

Set your scene up on the base, stopper or jar lid, then cover with the dome, globe or jar just to see how the placement looks. Remember that the dome sometimes acts as a magnifying glass, so you need to fool around with where you place the bits. When you're happy with the arrangement, use two-part epoxy or styrene-based adhesive sealant to glue things to the base. Experiment with model paints for painting the dome too. Paint the figures, scenery, background and dome base, jar lid or stopper; then let dry. If you want to use a photograph or paper memento as a background, cut out the desired image and, working quickly with a brush, coat all paper surfaces with two-part epoxy and let dry. (Just don't raid the family photo album without permission.)

3.

Liquid. If you use only water, it will expand and contract and possibly even break the dome, even if it's heated just from sitting on a sunny window sill. Fill one-half full with distilled water and add two to five ml (one-half to one tsp.) glycerine to the water to slow down the snow, retard algae growth, and decrease the likelihood of breakage. (You can buy glycerine at a drugstore.) Also add a tiny drop of detergent into the upturned globe.

4.

Add the snow. You want the snow to sink gently and retain its whiteness. You don't want it to clump or stick to objects. The key to perfect white snow is a very well-guarded secret. The earliest domes used bone chips, pottery flecks, porcelain, china chips, sand and wax bound with camphor. Ground-up shells work well, and the manufactured inexpensive domes use ground plastic. Sand works, but then you should use all glycerine and no water. Glitter is great for snow. You can choose white, silver or gold, and it floats nicely. Or pound thin white shells or disposable plastic cutlery into tiny pieces with a hammer. (Wear safety glasses.) Rinse in a strainer to remove dust before using. You could also try sequins, or cut up aluminum foil into glitter. Just experiment with the type of snow, and its "floatability," to know what kind and how much to add.

5.

Seal up the dome. Apply good-quality clear silicon (necessary because it will contract and expand and bend) around the inside edge of the recycled dome base or jar lid. Push the dome into the base or screw it onto the jar. Holding the globe or jar over a dishpan, work slowly, allowing the excess mixture to escape over the rim of the glass. (Be really careful with this step. When the figures and scenery are inserted into the mixture too quickly it is possible to break the glass.) If you are using a kit with a rubber stopper, don't apply glue to the stopper. Insert into the globe until the bottom of the stopper is flush.

To check for air bubbles, wait a few days before gluing a kit globe inside its wooden or plastic base. Remove the bubbles by tilting the globe, pulling the stopper away from one side and filling the globe with distilled water. Glue globe to base with glue gun.

When you display your snowdome, keep it out of strong sunlight and any other extremes of hot and cold.

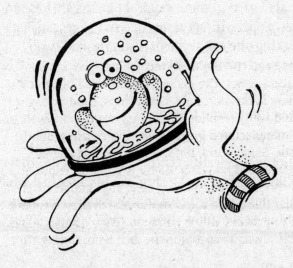

Why is Humpty Dumpty always shown as an egg when there is no egg mentioned anywhere in the rhyme?

Humpty Dumpty sat on a wall,

Humpty Dumpty had a great fall.

All the King's horses and all the King's men

Couldn't put Humpty together again.

There is an equivalent name for Humpty Dumpty in dozens of cultures: *gigele gagele, humpelken pumpelken, hillerin lillerin.*

Kate Greenaway, a children's illustrator, once drew Humpty Dumpty as a young child sitting on a high wall, dangling his legs, leaning forward and gazing into space with a forlorn expression. What happens to him seems worse if Humpty Dumpty is shown as a child. Normally he is portrayed as an egg with human characteristics. Why is that?

Maybe it has to do with superstition. Eggs occur in many mythological tales as creation symbols. They are also used in some magical practices. There are many superstitions associated with eggs (such as breaking one egg accidentally being bad luck). There's even an old rhyme:

Break an egg, break your leg,

Break three, woe to thee,

Break two, your love's true.

In the nineteenth century it was believed that having eggs on board a ship would cause bad winds that would blow you off course. Some fishermen wouldn't even allow them on their vessels. Even today there are people who believe strongly in brown over white eggs or vice versa, even though both colours are identical in food value. Some people believe that double yolks are lucky.

Is this egg superstition why Humpty Dumpty is portrayed as an egg? No. The fact that he's an egg is the answer to the rhyme's riddle. All the king's horses and all the king's men couldn't put Humpty together again because once an egg falls and breaks, it can't be repaired. This riddle is thousands of years old.

Little kids in lots of countries figure that when they dig a hole they are "digging to China." Where do kids in China think they will end up?

Nobody knows why we say we are digging to China. Maybe it is because until fairly recently, China seemed to be about as far away from North America as possible. There are lots of places in the world where children believe that they are digging to China: Canada, the United States, Australia, New Zealand and France, for starters. Childhood beliefs are pretty widespread.

None of this makes much sense — you can't dig through the earth because it's too hot in there. The earth has a molten interior, so if you dug straight down you'd get fried.

A person from China told me: "It's interesting to find out such an expression as 'digging to China.' When I was a kid, sometimes I told my friends we were heading for Brazil!" When he was older he realized that if he could go right through the earth from where he lived in southern China, he'd actually emerge in Chile . . . but that's pretty close to Brazil.

How do you figure out where you might emerge if you could dig straight through? For a rough idea, you could buy a cheap, small plastic globe and stick a knitting needle through it. But math comes to the rescue again. Look at a globe or an atlas for the latitudinal and longitudinal co-ordinates of where you live. For example, if you live in Toronto, the co-ordinates are 43 degrees 40 minutes north and 79 degrees 23 minutes west ($43°\ 40'$n, $79°\ 23'$w). The latitude part is simple, just the opposite of your starting point. For the longitude, though, you need this equation: $360° - (79°\ 23' + 180°)$. So, if you headed from Toronto straight through the centre of the earth, you would come out at $43°\ 40'$ south and $100°\ 37'$ east. (Remember that each degree is 60 minutes — that's why the $23°$ and $37'$ add up to $60'$, or $1°$.) Those co-ordinates would put you in the southern part of the Indian Ocean, about 1500 kilometres southwest of Perth, Australia. Not China.

If you live in Australia or somewhere else in the eastern hemisphere, you have to add a minus sign before the longitudinal co-ordinate when you do the calculation

Is it legal to do your income tax in Roman numerals?

People *can* do it, but the tax department doesn't really like it. (People who pull a stunt like this usually do it because they aren't happy about paying taxes. They just want to irritate the tax department.) If people do use Roman numerals, the income tax officials will pull out their form for "translation" and it will take extra time to have it processed, but it is, technically, legal.

The word taxation actually means "forced exaction." Taxes have been around for about 6000 years. There are Egyptian murals showing people being whipped for not paying their taxes. Throughout history people have not been amused about giving up a part of their wealth, no matter how happy they are about using the services their tax money pays for (like roads, schools, hospitals and water).

Apart from the Egyptian murals, another reason we know so much about taxation is the existence of the Rosetta Stone, from 200 B.C. It discusses how Egyptian king Ptolemy V reduced some taxes and abolished others.

In 1913 the United States joined a number of other countries which were already taxing incomes: Japan, New Zealand, Australia, the Netherlands and Germany. It took until 1917 for Canada to begin taxing personal income. Most governments consider income tax their single largest source of revenue.

Over the years the tax department has seen tax cheques written on all kinds of things — even a shirt. (Someone was obviously trying to make the point that the government was taking the "shirt off his back.") One person even sent in $4000.00 in coins. And then there was the time that a form came in with this note: "I don't you know why you should be interested in the length of my residence in Quebec, but I have nothing to hide. It is 10 metres long."

What's a stool pigeon?
and Origins of Other WEIRD WORDS AND PHRASES

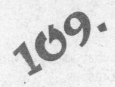

How do you say "the" in pig Latin?

Here's ow-hay. Let's learn with this phrase:

Remember, boys, you must not squelch, must not repress the urge to belch.

Pig Latin is a specific language with definite rules. Pig Latin works easily for most words. Just take off the first consonant, move it to the end of the word and add ay. For a word like "the," with two consonants at the beginning, move them both to the end. "The" becomes e-thay. "Urge" becomes urge-ay because it doesn't begin with a consonant. It sounds like gibberish, but it is gibberish with a pattern.

Emember-ray, oys-bay, ou-ay ust-may ot-nay

elch-squay, ust-may ot-nay epress-ray e-thay

urge-ay oo-tay elch-bay.

Pig Latin has been used since before World War I, primarily with school children. In 1933 Ginger Rogers recorded the song "We're in the Money" in Pig Latin, and that made it even more popular.

Secret languages are pretty terrific. (Ecret-say anguages-lay are-yay etty-pray errific-tay.) In back slang you just turn words backwards. The trick with back slang is putting the *name* of the first letter instead of the *sound*, to throw people off. . . T-ndluow T-aht K-conk R-uoy S-kcos F-fo. Check out the answer below.

WOULDN'T THAT KNOCK YOUR SOCKS OFF

149

Ayay Igpay Oempay:

Ethay itsyyay itsybay iderspay entway upyay
ethay aterway outspay,

Ownday amecay ethay ainray andyay
ashedway ethay iderspay outyay;

Outyay amecay ethay unsay andyay ashedway
awayyay ethay ainray,

Andyay ethay itsyyay itsybay iderspay entway
upyay ethay outspay againyay.

Can you make it out? It's the nursery rhyme, The
Itsy Bitsy Spider, in Pig Latin.

Get it? Good. Now try your name, your friends'
names, your grandparents', your little brothers'
and sisters', your teachers', anyone you can
think of! But beware, it's addictive, and you'll
find you keep thinking of everything in Pig
Latin! Eally-ray!

What does it mean to be dead as a doornail?

It means to be really dead. This is one of those
wacky sayings that, when you really think about it,
makes very little sense.

Why a doornail? What is a doornail? In earlier
times, not iron nails but hardwood pegs called
treenails were used in building houses and ships.
Iron nails used to be made by hand, a laborious and
therefore expensive process, so they were used only
where they had to be — doors, for example, because
they got so much use being opened and shut. People
would drive a nail in really hard, then bang down
the head. Because of this the nail could never be
used again, so these were "dead" doornails.

What's a stool pigeon?

Someone who squeals, tattles, spies, informs on or betrays another is called a stool pigeon. But why?

Pigeon meat was a real treat for the British, but shooting pigeons did so much damage the birds wouldn't be edible. The solution: Pigeons were lured into a trap by using another bird as a decoy.

The decoy bird sometimes had its eyes sewn shut, and was tied to the small stool that trappers sat on while they waited. The distressed bird would cry out to the others, who would come and get caught in the trap. So a "stool pigeon," now sometimes called a "stoolie," is something that lures its companions into being caught, betraying its own species.

How are you supposed to sleep tight?

This expression comes from the eighteenth and nineteenth centuries. Mattresses used to have rope supports rather than the box springs or wire bases of today. A feather mattress would sit on a rope base, with the rope woven in and out of holes in the bed frame. The ropes would sometimes have to be tightened so the mattresses wouldn't sag. People would say "sleep tight," referring to the ropes — that is, hoping that they would be tied tightly so that the sleeper would have a good night's rest.

What does it mean to be one brick short of a load?

No one is sure how or even when this expression originated, but it has come to be very popular. We all know that it is not polite to call someone stupid. So we sometimes use a "euphemism," a nicer expression that actually says something not so nice. One brick short of a load means that someone is not terribly bright. Not all there. Incomplete, like a load of bricks less one.

Some other expressions use similes to say more or less the same thing:

has a photographic memory, but the lens cap
  is on

the elevator doesn't quite make it to the
  top floor

a few clowns short of a circus

not the brightest bulb on the tree

as smart as bait

not the sharpest knife in the drawer

sharp as a marble

the lights are on, but nobody's home

you can look in one ear and see out of the other

bright as Alaska in December

a few noodles short of a casserole

Why is someone called mad as a hatter?

This is mad as in crazy, not mad as in angry. So what's a crazy hatter? A hatter is someone who makes hats. When they were made of wool or beaver pelts, they were felted (to make the fibres matted and dense) with a chemical called nitrate of mercury. Inhaling this nasty stuff could give a hat-maker brain damage, and make him seem quite mad.

In Lewis Carroll's *Alice in Wonderland* there is a Mad Hatter who wears a top hat, and acts really odd. It isn't known if the character was meant to be someone who had actually incurred brain damage, or if Carroll had modelled the character on a particular person who wore a top hat and acted eccentric. But Carroll's book certainly popularized the term Mad Hatter.

Now *you* try one:

Why do our noses run and our feet smell?

Why are boxing rings square?

Why do ships carry cargoes and cars carry shipments?

If you want to submit a challenging question for possible inclusion in a new book by Marg Meikle, e-mail it to: mmeikle@home.com or snail mail it to: c/o Funny You Should Ask, Publishing Division, Scholastic Canada Ltd., 175 Hillmount Road, Markham, Ontario L6C 1Z7.

Photo by Lionel Trudel

115.

How did you become known as The Answer Lady?

For over eight years I had the role of The Answer Lady on CBC Radio's *Gabereau* show. To get the audiences to participate, I encouraged people to ask me their wackiest questions. Each one (like "What does the Queen carry in her handbag?") made a great starting point.

How do I find my answers? The Internet, the library, a CD-ROM database, making a phone call to an expert — whatever it takes.

I've written several books: *Dear Answer Lady, Return of the Answer Lady, Bumbering Around Vancouver* and *Dog City: Vancouver.*

And where do I live? In Vancouver, B.C., with my husband Noel, new baby Mac, and dog Rosie.

Acknowledgements

Thanks to the following folks for help and support in my constant quests for answers:

Dr. Sue Albert, Rona Blackwood (RSPCA), Sandy Bogart Johnston, Ed Cavell, Dr. Stan Coren, Dr. Sue Crawford, Dr. Joel Ehrenkranz, Dr. John Elliott, Shannon Elliott, Vicki Gabereau, Margy Gilmour, Dr. Mary Ingraham, Heather Kennedy, Anne Lambert, Dr. Anne Macdonald, Noel MacDonald, Dr. Heather Meikle, Dr. Alexandra Palmer, Dr. Bob Phillips, Prince of Wales Northern Heritage Centre, Mr. Smarty Pants of *The Austin Chronicle*, Sheila Peacock, Ulrike Radermacher, Bill Richardson, Joe Rubin, Carolyn Swayze, Bob Teaffe (Rodeo Marketing Consultant), Doug Tuck, the librarians at the Vancouver Public Library, Rhiannon and Rory Vining, Sue Wagner, Karen Young.